Brighton & ...
BUS NAM...

Mike Cheesman
&
Adam Trimingham

POMEGRANATE PRESS

This book is dedicated to Jim Jones 1944–2000
(left in picture, with Mike Cheesman)
whose inspiration lives on in Brighton & Hove Buses

© Brighton & Hove Bus and Coach Company, 2004
Text by Adam Trimingham
Edited by Mike Cheesman

Cover photograph by Roger Bamber: Sheila Hobden, widow of the late Dennis Hobden
    (*see page 66*). 'I'm highly delighted to see Den remembered on a bus,' she said. 'He was
    the father of the town, and it's a great honour to see him remembered this way.'
Photograph on this page: Frank Stevens

Published by Pomegranate Press
51 St Nicholas Lane, Lewes, Sussex BN7 2JZ
email: pomegranatepress@aol.com
www.pomegranate-press.co.uk

ISBN 0-9542587-8-9

British Library Cataloguing-in-Publication Data.
A catalogue record for this book is available from the British Library

Printed by Cliffe Enterprise, 112 Malling Street, Lewes, East Sussex BN7 2RJ
Telephone: 01273 483890

Introduction

Brighton and Hove have always been places of innovation and interest. The ancient name for Brighton was Brighthelmstone, and in the Domesday Book it is mentioned under the name of Bristelmestune. The change of spelling to Brighton was officially adopted in the mid-19th century in a charter of incorporation.

Throughout history many famous people have passed through the city. Some stayed for just a short while (such as the future King Charles II for a single night in October 1651) while others spent their whole lives here.

Brighton & Hove Bus and Coach Company's ancestors can be traced back to 1884, and we are proud of our long association with the area. When the new double-deck buses were delivered in 1999 the company's operations director, Paul Williams, came up with the idea of naming them after notable landmarks. Like all good ideas, once it had been nurtured it became even better – in this case by using bus fronts to honour all the notable names from our local history. The main criteria for inclusion is that the person made a significant contribution to the area during his or her lifetime and is now deceased.

Little did we know the huge interest this would create over the next five years, to the extent that this book has become necessary to meet the many requests we receive for more information about all the names now 'on the buses'.

The first to be featured was King Charles II on a brand new Dennis Trident double-deck bus, fleet number 801. Twenty such buses were delivered and named between March and May 1999, with 18 of them allocated to the METRO Line 1 service between Whitehawk, City Centre, Hove, Portslade and Mile Oak. The other two were convertible open-top buses which operated on a variety of routes.

In September 1999 Brighton Marina started work on a Hollywood-style Walk of Fame featuring the many celebrities associated with Brighton and Hove. To coincide with this plan all the single-deck buses on METRO Line 7, which runs to the Marina, had names added from the Walk of Fame. Many of the celebrities featured are still alive and have been photographed with their bus. The actual Walk of Fame was launched two years later in 2001, and more recently these names have been sold from the bus fleet to be replaced on the Marina bus route with many of the first 20 double-decks already named. So the celebrities have gained a paving stone but lost a bus.

This book gives details, and pictures where possible, of all the famous and not so famous names featured on our buses from 1999 to summer 2004. Each page describes how that person has been involved in the development of Brighton and Hove.

Since 1999, 112 buses have been named as new double-decks have entered the fleet each year. Twenty more Dennis Tridents were delivered in 2000, with 24 in 2001 and 12 in 2002. In both 2003 and 2004 20 Scanias have arrived, with the last 20 sporting a brand new livery design and logo for the company, with more planned for delivery in the autumn.

Over the years other names have been added to certain buses to mark special events. Most interesting have been the results of bidding at charity acutions for a name to be shown on a bus – raising many thousands of pounds for good causes in the process. In April 2002 a bus was even named after a police dog after a public outcry over its passing.

In this book we have also included photographs of bus names that changed or had errors corrected after their initial display. We have, for instance, unwittingly omitted the occasional Sir on certain buses, as well as committing some gremlin spellings before someone has kindly pointed out the error. All are here as a complete compendium of the names featured on Brighton & Hove's buses.

The book is laid out in alphabetical order of the featured name with each page confirming the bus number and name, with photographs of the bus in service, and giving details of the person featured, a close up of their name, a photograph where possible and a summary of their achievements.

With more than a hundred personalities featured, this book is a history lesson of Brighton and Hove and its many notable characters. New buses will keep coming, and more names will be featured. We have a list of suggestions for names of buses pending – enough to keep us going for a few years – but if you can suggest any that you think we should feature, be sure to let us know. They are always gratefully received.

Many thanks to Adam Trimingham for helping to write this book (all but the last entry) and for providing the background to all the people featured; to Kevin Bacon of Brighton History Centre and to Kate Elliott of the *Argus* for searching out some of the images; to Godfrey Gould for checking through the details; to David Arscott for helping us with the production and distribution; to many others who I pestered for photos; and of course to my wife Julia for putting up with my dedication to get this book finished.

Mike Cheesman
August 2004

Photographic acknowledgements

Our thanks to the following for permission to use illustrative material. We have attempted to trace all copyright holders and will be pleased to rectify any omissions in future reprints.

Argus newspaper: pp 1 [819 on tour, Micky Adams and Bobby Zamora], 2 [Pietro Addis], 5 [Albion team, 820 on tour], 18 [Bruce, Roger French with Bruce bus], 20 [Dora Bryan], 45 [Chris Eubank], 47 [Adam Faith], 66 [Dennis Hobden], 70 [Derek Jameson], 91 [Moody].
Brighton-Net.com pp 75 [Roedean School], 104 [Clayton Tunnel].
Gordon Dinnage, Dtp Library: p 84 [Brighton Tram].
Chris Horlock for supplying photographs from his extensive archive.
Royal Pavilion, Libraries and Museums (Brighton and Hove): pp 17 [Sir Stanley Brown], 41 [Stanley Deason], 63 [Captain Henry Hill], 86 [Alan Melville], 88 [Herbert Menges], 92 [Dr Clifford Musgrave], 98 [Cecil Pashley], 101 [Margaret Powell], 107 [Dr Richard Russell], 116 [Dorothy Stringer], 117 [Stroudley locomotive], 119 [Stanley Theobald], 26 [Arthur Wagner].
St Dunstan's Archive, London: p 99 [Sir Arthur Pearson].
Most of the bus pictures were taken by Mike Cheesman, Mervyn Steadman and John Nicholas.

Ten more new Scania Omnidekkas arrived in September 2004 and are as follows: 637 Kenneth Bredon, 638 Sir Anton Dolin, 639 Raymond Francis, 640 Graham Greene, 641 John Jackson, 642 Howard Johnson, 643 Victoria Lidiard, 644 K.S. Ranjitsinhji, 645 Paul Stonor and 646 Herbert Wilcox.

In order to see them all and to keep up to date with new additions, log on to our website at www.buses.co.uk

819 MICKY ADAMS/BOBBY ZAMORA

Several of our buses have been named in honour of local sporting personalities. The former 'Max Miller' was renamed in May 2001 to celebrate Brighton & Hove Albion's promotion to Division 2 of the Football League.

Manager Micky Adams (above) and free-scoring centre forward Bobby Zamora (below) were two of the Albion heroes in their promotion year.

Parading in triumph. The Albion team tour the city to greet their fans – in one of our buses, of course.

819 Dennis Trident convertible open topper – carried these names during May 2001 only.

771 PIETRO ADDIS

An auction for the Argus appeal in 2001 offered two opportunities for people to have their names on the front of a bus, so raising more than £5,000 for charity. Pietro Addis, the manager of Donatello's restaurant, was one of the successful bidders.

771 Scania Cityzen – carried the name from October 2001 until August 2002.

821 QUEEN ADELAIDE

She was the wife of William IV, who succeeded his brother George IV and, like him, made some use of the Royal Pavilion. The couple were popular in Brighton and made regular visits until the king's death after only seven years on the throne.

When dowager queen she was the first monarch in the world to travel by train. Her little railway carriage, especially adapted with a small extension for her feet so that she could travel overnight, is still preserved at the National Railway Museum. Queen's Park in Brighton and Adelaide Crescent in Hove are named after her.

**Adelaide Crescent –
named after the queen.**

**Dennis Trident – has carried
the name since delivery in
March 2000.**

822 WILLIAM AINSWORTH

Usually known as Harrison Ainsworth, he was highly regarded in the Victorian era as a prolific writer of historical novels. He was born in 1805 but went out of fashion even before his death in 1882, and he has never been revived. His best known book, *Ovingdean Grange: a tale of the South Downs*, relates the flight and 'great escape' through Sussex of Charles II.

The Grange itself still stands in the village of Ovingdean. It used to be run by Brighton Council, but it is now privately owned.

822 Dennis Trident – has carried the name since delivery in March 2000.

820 THE ALBION TEAM 2001/2

Although Micky Adams and Bobby Zamora were given special treatment when the Albion were promoted to Division 2 the whole Albion team featured a year later as a celebration of their becoming champions of the division.

820 Dennis Trident convertible open-topper – carried the name during May 2002 only.

1 LORD ATTENBOROUGH

'Dickie' Attenborough played Pinkie Brown in the famous film version of Graham Greene's *Brighton Rock* and directed *Oh What a Lovely War!*, filmed on the West Pier.

He was also president of the Brighton Festival and chancellor of the University of Sussex.

1 Dennis Dart – carried the name from September 1999, on METRO line 7, until April 2004. The bus was sold in August 2004.

841 THOMAS ATTREE

In the early nineteenth century there were few more powerful figures than Thomas Attree. He was the son of William Attree, clerk to the commissioners and also vestry clerk. Sir Charles Barry designed for him the Italianate villa in Queen's Park (*below*), later known as Attree House. This magnificent villa, which eventually became a private school for the Xaverian order, was sadly demolished in 1970. Attree also bought the whole of Brighton Park in the east of the town, and with the permission of William IV called it Queen's Park after Queen Adelaide. The name remains today.

841 Dennis Trident – carried name since delivery in March 2001 on METRO Line 5.

601 WILLIAM ATTREE

He set up a legal practice in Ship Street that carried out much of the business in the town. William Attree also became clerk to the town commissioners (forerunners of the council) and vestry clerk. He negotiated the buying of land for the Royal Pavilion for both the Prince of Wales, later King George IV, and for William IV.

Attree, who was known as the King of Brighton, was also lord of the manor of Atlingworth and the official distributor of stamps for Surrey and Sussex. With Rev Edward Everard, he held the joint position of honorary secretary of the new Royal Sussex County Hospital in Eastern Road.

601 Scania Omnidekka – carried name since delivery in June 2003.

602 ENID BAGNOLD

The author of *National Velvet* lived for more than 50 years at North End House in Rottingdean, the house originally bought by Sir William Nicholson in 1920. Later Enid and her husband bought The Elms, Kipling's old house. Her play was made into a film starring Elizabeth Taylor in one of her first roles. Bagnold also wrote *The Chalk Garden*, which is still often performed today: it is clear from the stage directions that it was set in Rottingdean.

Described by contemporaries as dark and intelligent, Bagnold claimed to have been deflowered by the notorious rake Frank Harris. Altogether she wrote seven novels and nine plays. She also wrote books for children. Enid Bagnold was known in the village as Lady Jones, as she was married to the

proprietor of Reuters, Sir Roderick Jones. She was part of the Rottingdean set but she was dismissive of Rudyard Kipling, describing him as a little man whom nobody knew well. She died aged 91 in 1981.

602 Scania Omnidekka – carried name since delivery in June 2003.

The energetic and charismatic Bamber made his money through business deals before turning his attention to Brighton & Hove Albion, a team then permanently in the lower divisions of the Football League. Under his astute guidance Albion were promoted to the First Division (now the Premiership) and found greater glory by reaching the 1983 Cup Final. Albion almost won that match, which ended in a 2-2 draw, but they lost the replay against Manchester United 4–0. Things were never as good again. Albion were relegated and Bamber left the club, dying at an early age from cancer.

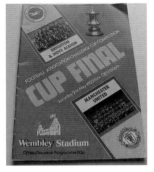

823 Dennis Trident – carried name since delivery in March 2000.

809 SIR CHARLES BARRY

Best known for designing the House of Parliament, Barry was also responsible for several fine buildings in Brighton. When a young man he won a competition to design what is now the parish church of St Peter's in York Place. Barry also designed the early buildings, now listed, at the Royal Sussex County Hospital in Eastern Road. Perhaps the most charming of his Brighton buildings is the Italianate church of St Andrew's in Waterloo Street, Hove, now closed for worship but open regularly to the public for viewing.

809 Dennis Trident – carried name since delivery in April 1999, originally on METRO Line 1, then METRO Line 7 from April 2004.

603 AUBREY BEARDSLEY

Few people have achieved so much in so short a time as Aubrey Beardley, who died from TB when he was only 25. Born in 1872 at Buckingham Road in Brighton, he died in 1898 at Menton, near Monte Carlo.

After attending Brighton Grammar School, Beardsley worked as a city clerk, but on the advice of Sir Edward Burne-Jones he took up art full time. His distinctive work in black and white made him one of the best known practitioners of Art Nouveau. He achieved notoriety by illustrating Oscar Wilde's *Salome*, and he also illustrated Dent's edition of *Morte d'Arthur* and both *The Yellow Book* and *The Studio*.

Although tainted by his association with Wilde, his reputation later recovered through his beautiful religious drawings. He was received into the Roman Catholic church in the year before his death.

603 Scania Omnidekka – carried name since delivery in June 2003.

Below right: the vehicle was orginally named Aubrey Beardlsey in error during June 2003.

842 EUGENIUS BIRCH

This great Victorian engineer and designer left Brighton with two major examples of his work. The West Pier, built in 1866 and completed in stages up to 1916, was designed by Birch opposite Regency Square despite opposition from neighbours. Now a sad wreck, thanks to neglect and arson, is has been described as the finest pleasure pier ever built, and is one

of only two to have been granted Grade I listed status. In 1871 Birch also built the Aquarium, then the largest in the world: today it's the Sea Life Centre. He designed a number of piers in other parts of England, including the north pier at Blackpool.

The West Pier in its heyday.

842 Dennis Trident – carried name since delivery in March 2001 on METRO Line 5.

619 MARGARET BONDFIELD

Born in Somerset in 1873, Margaret Bondfield was the 11th child in her family. Her father William, 61 at the time, was a textile worker well known for his radical political beliefs. The young Margaret became apprenticed at the age of 14 to a draper's store in Western Road, Brighton, and became friendly with one of her customers – Louise Martindale, a strong advocate of women's rights. Margaret was a regular visitor to the Martindale home, where she met other radicals living in Brighton.

Margaret went to London and became a member of the shop assistants union. In 1898 she created a storm by describing the ideal married couple as one in which both went out to work and shared the household tasks at home. She became secretary of the Women's Labour League, and in 1910 she persuaded the Liberal Government to include maternity benefits in its health insurance bill. She also campaigned for full voting rights for women

and opposed the first world war, wanting a negotiated peace with Germany.

In 1923 she became one of the first women MPs, joining the government the following year. In Ramsay Macdonald's second government in 1929 she became Minister of Labour – the first woman to gain a place in a British cabinet. She lost her seat in the 1931 election and the Labour party never forgave her for supporting Macdonald's National Government. She died in 1953.

619 Scania Omnidekka – carried name since delivery in February 2004 on METRO Line 1

865 & 866 BRIDE & GROOM

Originally named Queen Elizabeth II and Prince Philip, and painted in Golden Jubilee livery, both these buses were re-named Bride & Groom and used for private hire for weddings.

865 Dennis Trident – delivered in April 2002 in gold livery to celebrate the Queen's jubilee and renamed in January 2003. Both have now been repainted into the new livery and renamed Dusty Springfield (865) and Alan Weeks (866).

In the *Argus* Appeal of 2002 more than £3,000 was raised for charity through the auctioning of two bus names. Bridges Residential were the highest bidder, but unfortunately did not choose an individual's name for display on the front of the bus.

The company's headquarters in Western Road, Hove.

781 Scania Cityzen – carried name from October 2002 until September 2003.

815 SIR SAMUEL BROWN

The first pleasure pier in Brighton was at Brighton, and it was designed by Sir Samuel Brown. He had retired after a fine career in the Navy, and was a specialist both in naval architecture and marine engineering. Usually known as Captain Brown, he was

a pioneer in the use of cables and had already built the Union Bridge across the Tweed and designed the ironwork for Hammersmith Bridge in London. He used help from Thomas Telford for the Chain Pier, and Telford used his expertise in turn for the Menai Straits Bridge in Wales.

The pier, a landing stage that was also used as a promenade, collapsed in a storm in 1896.

Above: The Chain Pier, which opened in 1823.

Below: 815 Dennis Trident – carried name since delivery in May 1999. Originally on METRO Line 1, then repainted into normal red livery from March 2002.

Bottom right: The name was at first mistakenly used without the 'Sir' prefix.

12 BRUCE

Brighton police dog Bruce was put down in April 2002 after biting an offender's ear. A huge public outcry led to his name being displayed on a bus at short notice. Luckily Brighton & Hove were able to put it together quickly in response to suggestions from the *Argus* newspaper because they had a spare 'Chris Eubank' name in the office and the letters B-R-U-C-E could easily be cut from this!

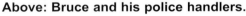

Above: Bruce and his police handlers.

Left: Bus company managing director Roger French with the renamed vehicle – 'DOG' on the destination board and 'BRUCE' on the facia below the window.

Below: 12 Dennis Dart – carried name between April and May 2002.

844 CAROLINE OF BRUNSWICK

The true love of George IV while he was Prince of Wales was Maria Fitzherbert, but he could not legally marry her because she was a Roman Catholic. In 1795 he decided to marry his cousin, Princess Caroline of Brunswick, but their union was far from a success. He was said to find her repellently ugly, while she was not taken with the prince and his autocratic ways.

They came to Brighton after their wedding and stayed at what is now Marlborough House in the Old Steine. Their daughter Charlotte was born the following year, but soon afterwards the couple separated. At his coronation in 1821 Charlotte was refused access to the ceremony at Westminster Abbey.

844 Dennis Trident – carried name since delivery in March 2001 on METRO Line 5.

2 DORA BRYAN

Although she is best known for starring in musicals and revues, Dora Bryan won an Olivier award for straight acting roles in *A Taste of Honey* and *She Stoops to Conquer*. She has been a resident of Brighton more more than 30 years.

2 Dennis Dart – carried name from September 1999, on METRO Line 7 until April 2004. The bus was sold in August 2004.

620 OLIVER BULLEID

Born in New Zealand in 1882, and usually know as O.V.S. Bulleid, he was one of the innovators of locomotive design. His is remembered by railway enthusiasts as a forward-thinking mechanical engineer to the old Southern Railway: the Bulleid Society celebrated his centenary with a two-day country fair at Horsted Keynes station on the restored Bluebell Railway.

Bulleid designed the famous West Country, Battle of Britain and Merchant Navy class of locomotives. The Battle of Britain class Fighter Command was the 1,000th engine to be built at the locomotive works in Brighton and was named at a special ceremony at Brighton station in 1947 with Air Vice Marshall Keith Park and fighter ace Douglas Bader present.

He died in 1972 at the age of 90. More than 30 of his locomotives still exist today.

A Battle of Britain class locomotive, designed by Oliver Bulleid.

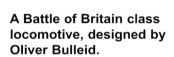

620 Scania Omnidekka – carried name since delivery in March 2004, on METRO Line 1.

604 SIR EDWARD BURNE-JONES

One of the most famous artists of his day, Sir Edward Burne-Jones lived for many years in Rottingdean. In 1880 he merged Prospect Cottage and Aubrey Cottage, which faced The Green, and renamed them North End House. (The house has now been divided once again.)

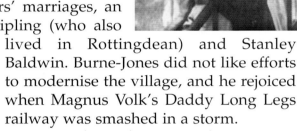

Burne-Jones became famous in the 1870s. He was a great friend of William Morris until the latter's death in 1896. He had a great eye for colour and a command of line, and many of his subjects had literary allusions.

He married Georgina MacDonald in 1860 and later became, through his sisters' marriages, an uncle to their sons Rudyard Kipling (who also

North End House, Rottingdean.

lived in Rottingdean) and Stanley Baldwin. Burne-Jones did not like efforts to modernise the village, and he rejoiced when Magnus Volk's Daddy Long Legs railway was smashed in a storm.

His work can be seen today in many galleries and in local churches, including St Paul's in West Street, the Church of the Annunciation in Washington Street and St Margaret's in Rottingdean.

**604 Scania Omnidekka –
carried name since delivery in
June 2003.**

He was the first man to have become mayor of Brighton two, and then three times, and was highly regarded by the people as well as by his fellow councillors. Born in Ipswich in 1813, he became a surgeon and arrived

here in 1837. He joined the council in 1854 and his first spell as mayor began only three years later. He chose the town's motto *In Deo Fidemus* (In God We Trust). He opened the Aquarium during his third term as mayor in 1871, and paid for part of the Victoria Fountain in Old Steine. He was nicknamed King Cordy because of his influence, and when he died in 1876 as many as 30,000 mourners lined the streets. Two years later a statue was unveiled to him in the grounds of the Royal Pavilion. It was moved to the south of the Old Steine in 1984 when the Pavilion grounds were redesigned.

The statue of 'King Cordy' south of the Old Steine.

843 Dennis Trident – carried name since delivery in March 2001 on METRO Line 5.

Great buildings need great architects, and Brighton was fortunate to be served by a man with the talent of Charles Busby. With his builder partner Amon Wilds, Busby built many of the great Regency squares and crescents in Kemp Town and Hove which contain most of the city's top listed buildings. Busby and Wilds also built a great many individual houses in many parts of Brighton.

Born in 1788, Busby published several books on architecture. He lived at Waterloo Place in Brighton and Lansdowne Place in Hove. He died in 1834 and is buried in St Andrew's church.

St Margaret's Chapel – designed by Charles Busby.

824 Dennis Trident – carried name since delivery in March 2000.

839 FRANK BUTTERWORTH

840 IAN CALDWELL

Brighton & Hove buses' awards evening in 2001 offered staff two chances to bid for the prestige of having their names on the buses – an event which raised £1700 for charity.

One was won by Lewes Road driver Frank Butterworth (*right*). The other was Ian Caldwell

(*below*), who had been declared 'personality of the year' by Peter Salvage, his manager.

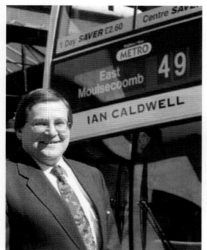

839 and 840 Dennis Tridents – carried names during April 2001 only on METRO Line 49.

816 SIR HERBERT CARDEN

The maker of modern Brighton was a solicitor who served as mayor during part of the first world war. A socialist in a Tory town, Sir Herbert Carden was much respected by his colleagues for his forward thinking. He was keen to preserve the Downs, both from development and as a water catchment area. He bought land when it became available and then sold it to the Corporation at cost price. In this way Brighton was able to build up a downland holding of more than 10,000 acres, including land in neighbouring districts such as what is now Lewes.

Carden served on the council from 1895 until his death in 1941. He was made a freeman of the borough and knighted for his services to Brighton. Thanks to his energy and commitment, Brighton became a pioneer in such matters as trams, telephones, electricity, road widening and housing. He also paid half the £2000 cost of erecting the

Carden paid half the cost of the Pylons on the A23.

Pylons north of Patcham on the A23 to commemorate the expansion of Brighton's boundaries in 1928.

816 Dennis Trident – carried name since delivery in May 1999. Originally *(below)* named Herbert Carden, the Sir being added in July 1999. First on METRO Line 1, then repainted into new METRO Line 1 livery from April 2004.

801 KING CHARLES II

The future king spent only one night in Brighton (October 14th/15th 1651) and therefore had the briefest local connection of anyone who is commemorated on our buses. Fleeing from the Battle of Worcester in the Civil War, Charles arrived at the Sussex coast. Here he found Captain Nicholas Tettersell, who was prepared to help him – although he upped the price from £60 to £200 when he discovered the identity of his passenger. In Tettersell's coal brig *Surprise*, later renamed *The Royal Escape*, Charles made his getaway to France. He later returned in triumph to start his reign as king in 1660  (Tettersell was rewarded), and he remained on the throne until 1865. A yachting race is staged each year off the Brighton coast to commemorate these events.

A re-enactment of the Battle of Worcester.

801 Dennis Trident – carried name since delivery in March 1999. Originally on METRO Line 1, then METRO Line 7 from April 2004.

845 QUEEN CHARLOTTE

She was the wife of George III and the mother of George IV. On several occasions she came to Brighton and visited the Royal Pavilion which had been built by her son. On one occasion she was so delighted by its appearance that she contributed £50,000 of her own money towards it – a huge sum in those days. The old queen was heartbroken when her granddaughter Princes Charlotte died in childbirth in 1817. She said of her suffering son: 'He can have nothing to reproach himself with, but can say with truth that he made her happy.' She is the queen referred to in the name of the King & Queen pub in Marlborough Place.

Above: The King & Queen pub in Marlborough Place.

Right: 845 Dennis Trident – carried name since delivery in March 2001 on METRO Line 5.

605 ELLEN NYE CHART

Henry Nye Chart took over the Theatre Royal in Brighton in 1854, built a new auditorium and played most of the leading roles in his productions there. In 1865 a young actress called Ellen Rollason made her debut in the company and was an immediate success in productions such as *The School for Scandal*. Two years later they married and were a successful duo in Brighton. When Nye Chart died in 1875 his widow took over and started a period of remarkable brilliance for the theatre. Local casts were often replaced by West End stars. At Christmas time many comedians destined to find fame and fortune in

London appeared in Theatre Royal pantomimes. Great actresses such as Ellen Terry and Mrs Patrick Campbell appeared at the Royal, while the actors included Sir Henry Irving and Seymour Hicks. Mrs Chart died in 1892 and her ghost is said to haunt the historic theatre.

The Theatre Royal was revived by Ellen Nye Chart.

605 Scania Omnidekka – carried name since delivery in June 2003.

825 SIR WINSTON CHURCHILL

The celebrated wartime leader attended a school in Brunswick, Hove, when a small boy, and a plaque on a house wall in Lansdowne Place records the fact. His parents paid little attention to him when he was there and Churchill was often unhappy, at one time becoming seriously ill. He would worship at the Chapel Royal, steadfastly facing east while the rest of the congregation faced (incorrectly but logically) north.

Churchill went on to attend Harrow, where he failed to cover himself with scholastic glory. Later, however, he became a journalist, writer, MP and, of course, prime minister, leading Britain to victory against Hitler in 1945. In 1947 he was made an honorary freeman of the borough of Brighton. He died 18 years later, aged 90.

825 Dennis Trident – carried name since delivery in March 2000.

622 C.B. COCHRAN

O ne of the greatest showmen of the last century, C.B. Cochran was born in a house in Prestonville Road, Brighton, in 1872. He appeared in a show early in life with an unlikely duo – Sir Herbert Carden and Aubrey Beardsley. Cochran gained his appetite for show business after visiting a fair at Lindfield, near Haywards Heath. He decided he would like to be an actor after seeing a pantomime at the Theatre Royal in Brighton.

Cochran went to the USA as a poor young man and scraped a living there as a salesman and part-time actor. He returned to England and started his career as an impresario by promoting a boxing match at Olympia. Then he put on many more, including the Carpentier v Beckett fight at Holborn which netted him £30,000, and he introduced rodeo to Britain and roller-skating to France. But he had failures as well, and went bust in 1924.

Recovering, he had a long association with Noel Coward, putting on *Private Lives* and *Cavalcade* among other plays. He had a troop of lovelies known as C.B. Cochran's Young Ladies. His discoveries included Anna Neagle, Jessie Matthews and Florence Desmond. During his career he worked with such celebrities as Charlie Chaplin, George Bernard Shaw, Will Rogers and Richard Tauber. Cochran continued after the war with the musical *Bless the Bride*, his 126th production, which achieved his longest run. He died in 1951.

622 Scania Omnidekka – carried name since delivery in March 2004 on METRO Line 1.

818 LORD COHEN

The charismatic founder of the Alliance Building Society made it possible for thousands of ordinary people in Brighton and elsewhere to own their own homes. He teamed up with builders to put up houses in the suburbs of Brighton and Hove, and then offered people the finance to pay for them through mortgages.

Cohen, a socialist, was elected mayor by Tory Brighton Council and cut a flamboyant figure. Among his ambtious but unrealised ideas was a large music and entertainments pavilion on the front in 1949 which would also have included a conference hall, a dance hall, restaurants and a ballroom. Another was for a chain of gardens right through the town from Preston Park to the sea, which would have involved demolishing much property. He also mooted a continental bathing place on the beach near the West Pier.

Many of his ideas were ahead of their time, but had a lot of common sense as well as being visionary. Cohen also gave backing to the Theatre Royal during difficult times, especially in the years of the second world war. He was less successful in his bid to become MP for Brighton Kemp Town, losing to the equally colourful Tory MP Howard Johnson. Lord Cohen of Brighton made the Alliance into one of Britain's top ten building societies before his early death in the Sixties.

Two name changes before it was right!

818 Dennis Trident – carried name since delivery in May 1999. Originally named Lewis Cohen. Renamed Lord Lewis Cohen in July 1999, then changed to Lord Cohen in late July 1999. First on METRO Line 1, then repainted into new METRO Line 1 livery from May 2004.

846 CAPT. FREDERICK COLLINS

He operated his Skylark pleasure sailing boats from Brighton beach. His cry of 'Any more for the Skylark?!' was so famous that it became a national symbol of pleasure boating. Captain Collins volunteered his boats for the Dunkirk mission in 1940, and two of the three were lost.

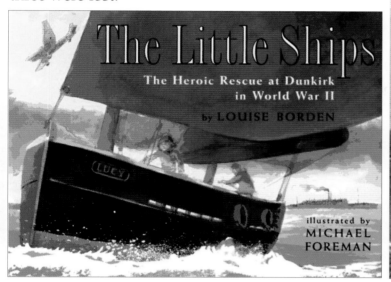

846 Dennis Trident – carried name since delivery in March 2001 on METRO Line 5.

621 IVY COMPTON-BURNETT

Born in Middlesex, she spent her childhood in Hove and lived for 18 years at The Drive, where there is a plaque to her. Ivy Compton-Burnett's father was a doctor whose first wife died in childbirth after producing six children.

His second wife, Ivy's mother Katherine, had another seven. The family had a pew at St John's church in Palmeira Square, although they attended other churches in Hove as well, including All Saints. Dr Burnett, a homeopath, published dozens of medical works and also built several homes in Hove before his sudden death at the age of 60 in 1901 when Ivy was nearly 17.

Ivy took a hand in managing the family affairs, including running farms, villas and building plots. She didn't like Hove, and called it 'a horrid, horrid place'. The house was not her favourite, either. Her first novel, *Dolores*, appeared in 1911, the year in which her mother died, but she did not like the work and it was another 14 years before her next book was published. She wrote 20 novels before her death in 1969, many of them with themes of homosexuality and incest. Lauded by her contemporaries, including Evelyn Waugh, she has now rather gone out of fashion.

621 Scania Omnidekka – carried name since delivery in February 2004 on METRO Line 1.

3 NORMAN COOK

The man behind Fat Boy Slim, the Housemartins and Beats International married Radio I's Zoe Ball. He studied in Brighton, lives in Hove and is a director of Brighton & Hove Albion. He organised a notoriously

all-too-successful beach party at Brighton in 2000 and vowed never to do it again.

Fat Boy Slim album.

3 Dennis Dart – carried name from September 1999 on METRO Line 7 until April 2004. The bus was sold in August 2004.

Every Brighton & Hove Albion fan has heard of the great goalscorers Peter Ward and Bobby Zamora, but the man who scored more league goals than anyone else in the club's history was Tommy Cook. In a remarkable career he scored 123 goals in only 209 appearances between 1921 and 1929. He scored more goals during another two seasons with Bristol Rovers. Born at Cuckfield in 1901, Cook was the first Albion player to be capped for England – against Wales in the 1924/25 season. Before then he had attended school in Brighton, and during the first world war as a seaman he received a medal for saving a life. On return to civvy street he became a structural engineer and a fitter before starting

Tommy Cook on a John Player cigarette card.

his soccer career. Cook also played cricket, which he preferred, scoring more than 20,000 runs for Sussex and taking 80 wickets. He made 32 centuries, and his highest score was 278. He came back to manage Albion after the second world war but lost his job after a bad run of results. Three years later, dogged with ill health, he took an overdose and died. He was 48.

623 Scania Omnidekka – carried name since delivery in March 2004, on METRO Line 1.

A man of many parts, Eric Courtney-King was perhaps best known for being chairman of Brighton & Hove Albion in the Sixties. His links with Albion began through the supporters' club. A wealthy businessman, he owned 30 dry-cleaning shops trading as Courtneys. He took on the chairman's role in 1963 when the club

Courtney-King (second left) with other Albion directors in the late 1960s. In the centre is actor/comedian Norman Wisdom.

Courtney-King House.

was in a parlous position, dropping into the fourth division. He appointed Archie Macaulay from West Bromwich Albion as manager. With a reconstituted board, including men with money such as Harold Paris, Macaulay was encouraged to spend on players and it paid off. Albion were unbeaten at home for a whole season and they won the championship. Courtney-King eventually left the board because of a spinal complaint which, typically, he did not reveal.

He established the Federation of Sussex Industries with the redoubtable Nora Potter. He was also a JP, a pominent member of Rotary and a freemason. He established many old people's lunch clubs in the area, and helped start the Brighton Festival. He died in 1999 aged 96.

624 Scania Omnidekka – carried name since delivery in February 2004 on METRO Line 1.

826 HARRY COWLEY

The champion of the ordinary man was born in Brighton and spent all his life here. A chimney sweep, he became indignant when, after both world wars, many servicemen were not properly housed in their own town. Cowley and his so-called Vigilantes occupied empty houses so that these men would have somewhere to live. He also ran the Upper Gardner Street market with a fist of iron and campaigned for the rights of traders. In the Thirties he led a successful fight against Oswald Mosley's fascists, who held meetings in the town. He also spent much time successfully arguing that three local men were innocent of a murder charge.

With his trademark bowler hat and tie, Cowley became one of the best known men in Brighton, and he continued to fight for causes until his death. In his later years he set himself up as the champion of old age pensioners, and he also joined squatters during their campaigns in the 1960s. Although on the side of working people, he never allied himself to any political party. People would know he was going to fight against an injustice when he declared: 'This don't come right to me'.

Called the Guv'nor, he attracted one of the largest crowds since the war for his funeral. On the coffin was a bowler hat in flowers.

826 Dennis Trident – carried name since delivery in March 2000. Originally in normal red livery, then repainted into METRO Line 49 livery from June 2003.

867 ARTHUR H COX

For 140 years the Arthur H. Cox pill factory was a familiar site in Brighton – an imposing building at the junction of Upper Lewes Road and Lewes Road. The firm eventually moved to north Devon to take advantage of the grants in a deprived area, and the factory was pulled down. It was replaced by the Sainsbury's superstore, which has echoes of the old factory in its design. Cox, an entreprenurial Victorian businessman, was also on Brighton Council and served a term as mayor. During that time he opened Preston Park.

An early Arthur H Cox chemist shop in Brighton.

867 Dennis Trident – carried name since delivery in April 2002. Originally named Arthur Cox (below), with the H added June 2002.

868 SYD DEAN

The Regent, built in Queen's Road in 1921, was the first super cinema in Brighton and could house 1700 people. Two years later a ballroom was opened next door in North Street, and it became an immediate success. Generations of Brightonians met there each week and enjoyed dancing on

its famous sprung floor. Bandleader Syd Dean was resident there during the 1940s and 1950s and was extremely popular. Dean, who lived in Hove, imposed strict discipline on the members and coaxed sweet sounds from them.

Above: Syd Dean (left) with members of his band.

Below: The Regency Ballroom.

The ballroom closed in the early 1970s, along with the cinema. Although there was an advertised replacement in the Top Rank Centre a few hundred yards down the road in West Street, somehow it was never the same. Rock 'n' roll had also dulled the public appetite for dance music, and although Dean tried many revivals his best days were by then over. Dapper and personable, he was a national figure who frequently broadcast on the BBC. He said of his fame in Brighton: 'There's Rottingdean, Saltdean – and Syd Dean.'

868 Dennis Trident – carried name since delivery in April 2002.

827 STANLEY DEASON

Brighton was a Tory town until 1986, but many of the great men it produced were socialists, and it says much for the Conservatives that they recognised this. One of them was Stanley Deason, a councillor and alderman from 1928 until his retirement in 1973 who was elected mayor in 1963. Deason helped restore the Royal Pavilion when millions of pounds were needed to restore the palace. He was passionately committed to

improved education,

and as a tribute a new school in east Brighton was named after him. After two name changes the school in Wilson Avenue is likely to close, but the nearby sports centre still bears Deason's name.

827 Dennis Trident – carried name since delivery in March 2000. Originally in normal red livery, then repainted into METRO Line 49 livery from April 2003.

828 CHARLES DICKENS

In the days before radio and TV, novelists were often stars, and when Dickens came to Brighton to give readings from his books he filled halls wherever he spoke – the largest of these in Victorian times being the big meeting room at

Brighton town hall. Dickens, whose works included *Great Expectations, The Pickwick Papers* and *David Copperfield*, had a strong sense of justice and often campaigned for the underdog. He stayed at the old Bedford Hotel, which was destroyed by fire in 1964.

828 Dennis Trident – carried name since delivery in March 2000. Originally in normal red livery, then repainted into METRO Line 49 livery from July 2003.

847 EARL OF EGREMONT

He was the lord who resided at Petworth House in West Sussex, one of the great mansions of England, now owned by the National Trust. Lord Egremont was one of a group of noblemen who established the first races at Brighton in 1783, and the racecourse is still there to this day. The artist J.M.W. Turner came to Brighton several times while staying with the earl at Petworth, where his descendants still live: some of his works, including a painting of the Chain Pier, are on display in the house. For a time the earl stayed at East Lodge in Brighton, and Egremont Place is named after him. He also helped establish the Royal Sussex County Hospital in Eastern Road in the 1820s.

847 Dennis Trident – carried name since delivery in March 2001 on METRO Line 5.

865 QUEEN ELIZABETH II

To celebrate the Queen's golden jubilee in 2002 two buses were painted in a gold livery.

865 Dennis Trident – carried name from April 2002 until January 2003, then renamed Bride & Groom.

4 CHRIS EUBANK

Like him or loathe him, you have to admit that he's a character. The former world boxing champion lives in Hove and supports local charities such as the Rocking Horse Appeal. He has also been involved in attempts to save the West Pier.

4 Dennis Dart – carried name from September 1999 on METRO Line 7 until April 2004. The bus was sold in October 2004.

848 SIR GEORGE EVEREST

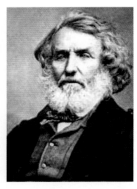

The man with one of the most famous names in the world is buried in Hove, and no one is really sure why. It could be that he wanted to be next to his eldest sister Licetta, but he lived in London and had no connection with the town. Everest took on the job of surveyor in India despite many attacks of fever, including malaria, which almost killed him. He revolutionised the way in which surveying was carried out, enabling the Himalayas to be measured accurately for the first time. Everest's name was given to the highest peak by his successor, Andrew Waugh. This was not a popular choice

among his staff, because many disliked his sarcastic manner and there was a feeling that the mountain should have a local name.

He retired in 1843 after 20 gruelling years in the job. He didn't marry until he was 56, and he was older than his father-in-law. He and his wife had six children in 10 years.

848 Dennis Trident – carried name since delivery in March 2001 on METRO Line 5.

6 ADAM FAITH

The singer and actor who first sprang to pop fame in the late 1950s had extensive business connections in Brighton. He lived and worked here in the 1970s when he co-managed Leo Sayer. He died in 2003.

6 Dennis Dart – carried name from September 1999 until April 2004 on METRO Line 7. The bus was sold in October 2004.

858 MALCOLM FARLEY

At the Brighton & Hove bus company awards evening in 2001 Dave Taylor, a Conway Street driver, was a successful bidder in an event which raised £1700 for charity. He dedicated a bus to Malcolm Farley, a

respected fellow driver who had lost his battle against cancer. The name was displayed for a month on a newly delivered bus.

Above: Malcolm Farley.

Right: Malcolm's children in front of Dad's bus.

Above left: Four successful bidders on the night. Left to right: Ian Caldwell, Dave Taylor, Peter Salvage and Frank Butterworth (*see also page 25*).

Left: 858 Dennis Trident – delivered in March 2001. Originally named Malcolm Farley during April 2001, then changed name in May 2001 on METRO Line 5.

606 TOMMY FARR

One of the greatest British boxers of the last century, Tommy Farr was the heavyweight champion of Great Britain. His finest moment came when he fought the world champion Joe Louis in 1937 in front of 37,000 people. Farr lost but was one of the few to have lasted a whole match with the Brown Bomber, and his fame was assured from that day on.

Welsh-born Farr had 296 fights, a fantastic number by today's standards, and was never punch-drunk. He lived in Sussex for many years, and when he retired from the ring he took over the Royal Standard pub in Queen's Road, Brighton. He lived in Old Fort Road, Shoreham, and took an active part in local affairs, being a prominent member of the Sussex Ex-Boxers Association. He retained the firmest handshake in Sussex right up to the time of his death in 1986 aged 71.

The Royal Standard pub in Queen's Road, Brighton, which Tommy Farr ran.

606 Scania Omnidekka – carried name since delivery in June 2003.

805 MARIA FITZHERBERT

Maria Fitzherbert was the morganatic, or unofficial, wife of George IV. They married in a secret ceremony in December 1785 – a union which could never be revealed because Mrs Fitzherbert, a widow twice over, was also a Roman Catholic. Still young, but now rich, she moved to Brighton, living in a fine house in the Old Steine which is now the YMCA: it was rumoured that there was a secret underground tunnel to the Royal Pavilion. The prince's passion later cooled. He married Caroline, whom he did not love, but he left Maria a handsome annuity and she was recognised by the next king, George's brother William IV, once he realised what had happened. Mrs Fitzherbert remained in Brighton after her break with George. She lived with two adopted daughters, and some

believed that the king was their father. She died in 1837 at the ripe old age of 80 and is buried at St John the Baptist church in Kemp Town.

Marlborough House, now the YMCA.

805 Dennis Trident – carried name since delivery in April 1999, originally on METRO Line 1, then METRO Line 7 from April 2004.

849 EDWIN FOWNES

Before the railways came to Sussex in the 1840s the best way to get about was by horse. Even though the roads in the Weald were notoriously muddy, it was possible to get down from London to Brighton in a few hours by coach and horse. Perhaps the most famous four-in-hand coachman was Edwin Fownes, born in 1851, who was based in Brighton. He retired in 1916 but didn't die until 1943, by which time all the horses used for transport had gone.

849 Dennis Trident – carried name since delivery in March 2001 on METRO Line 5.

625 WILLIAM FRIESE-GREENE

The great film pioneer was born in Bristol in 1855 and was apprenticed to a photographer. In 1887 he invented a moving picture to great acclaim, applying for a patent two years later. He opened a number of studios, including one in Brighton.

The plaque in Worcester Villas.

Friese-Greene led a chaotic life and was declared bankrupt three times because he was hopeless with finance: he went to prison at least once for debt. He took out a patent for cinematography in natural colours in 1905 and started a company based in Western Road. He founded another laboratory in Middle Street, where there is a plaque to him. There is another in Worcester Villas, Hove, where Friese-Greene lived with his wife and six children in the early years of the last century. Sadly his youngest child, Raymond, was kicked to death by a horse while playing in the street, and the family had to leave after his third bankruptcy. He was involved in lengthy legal disputes with other film pioneers in the area, included George Albert Smith, which did none of them any good. He lived in penury for the rest of his life, and although friends started a fund to support him it failed to raise much money. He died after speaking at a meeting on London in 1921 – his subject, ironically, being unity in the film trade.

625 Scania Omnidekka – carried name since delivery in February 2004 on METRO Line 1.

829 C.B. FRY

It would be impossible now for one man to display his sporting talents in so many arenas. Charles Burgess Fry held the world long jump record and appeared in an FA Cup Final. He also played rugby for Oxford, Blackheath and the Barbarians, and could have played for England. At Oxford he won 12 blues and captained the university at cricket, soccer and athletics in the same year. But his main passion was cricket, and he captained both Sussex and England. He held several records, including scoring the most centuries in a row. When he was captain of England he never lost a Test.

Fry had a colourful life outside sport and was once offered the throne of Albania, which he declined. He wrote both a novel and an autobiography and became an influential journalist. He entered politics as a Liberal, was involved with Baden-Powell and the Scouts and ran a training ship for youngsters. Going to Hollywood, he almost became a film star, and he met many of the top names there, including Boris Karloff. He lived long enough to appear on television.

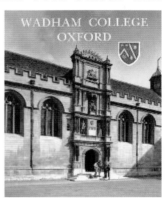

Wadham College, where Fry graduated.

829 Dennis Trident – carried name since delivery in March 2000. Originally on METRO Line 1, then METRO Line 7 from April 2004 and into the new livery from May 2004.

626 LORD FULTON OF FALMER

John Scott Fulton had a remarkable career in public life and is best known in Sussex for being a founder of the university at Falmer. Many others claimed to have had the idea, but Fulton was certainly the man most involved, becoming the first vice chancellor of the University of Sussex in the early days, when it had modest headquarters in Brighton. It expanded quickly, and in 1967 he handed over to his great friend

Professor Asa Briggs. Before coming to Sussex he had been vice chancellor of the University of Wales. Knighted in 1964, he became a life peer two years later.

Fulton was a BBC govenor and took an interest in ITV in the early years. He was also chairman of the British Council and president of the Society for Research into Higher Education. Taking the title Lord Fulton of Falmer, he eventually left the campus to conduct a full-scale enquiry into the civil service.

Falmer church and pond.

626 Scania Omnidekka – carried name since delivery in February 2004 on METRO Line 1.

775 TINA GOLDBERG-LOWE

David Goldberg-Lowe bid for one of two bus names at an auction for the *Argus* Appeal in 2002, an event which raised more than £3000 for charity. He chose his wife's name as a tribute to her memory.

775 Scania Cityzen – carried name from October 2002 until September 2003.

850 BARON GOLDSMID

In 1830 he bought the Wick estate in Hove, a large and valuable tract of land. It was developed into the Grade 1 buildings of Adelaide Crescent and Palmeira Square. Wick Hall in Furze Hill retains the name of the estate and there was a pub called the Wick in Holland Road. Goldsmid Road is named after him, and there is still a Goldsmid ward which returns three councillors to Brighton and Hove City Council.

Wick Hall.

Isaac Lyon Goldsmid was the first Jew to be created a baronet. After he settled a boundary dispute in South America (at the behest of Queen Victoria) he was created a baron in the Portuguese peerage, taking the title Baron da Goldsmid e da Palmeira. (Palmeira Square is also named after him.) After the baronetcy died out in the male line Queen Victoria agreed that it might continue through the female, one of his granddaughters having married Count Henry D'Avigdor – thus the Davigdor/Goldsmids. The names of several other members of the family can be found in Hove streets, among them Julian (the third baronet), Osmond (Sir Osmond Elim D'Avigdor-Goldsmid) and Montefiore – into which family another of Isaac's granddaughters married.

850 Dennis Trident – carried name since delivery in March 2001 on METRO Line 5.

806 MARTHA GUNN

When Brighton became fashionable in the eighteenth century the rich dame down to the beach to swim. Many of them had difficulty in getting across the hard, unyielding stones to reach the water. People called dippers help them into the water, and the most celebrated of them all was Martha Gunn.

Born in 1726, she worked for more than 60 years, eventually retiring through infirmity and ill health. The Prince of Wales was fond of her and granted her free access to his kitchen at the Royal Pavilion. She lived until 1815 and is buried in the churchyard of St Nicholas in Brighton. There is a portrait of her in the Pavilion.

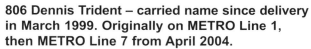

806 Dennis Trident – carried name since delivery in March 1999. Originally on METRO Line 1, then METRO Line 7 from April 2004.

8 SALLY GUNNELL

The locally-based Olympic athlete is the only woman in history to hold concurrently the Commonwealth, European, Olympic and World titles in the 400m hurdles. She trained at Withdean Stadium.

8 Dennis Dart – carried name from September 1999 on METRO Line 7 until April 2004. The bus was sold in August 2004.

808 LES HAMILTON

Starting from humble beginnings, and later working as an insurance agent, this true man of Portslade became one of the best-known politicians in the city of Brighton and Hove. He was elected to the Portslade urban council in 1958 and became its chairman six years later. When Hove took over Portslade in 1974 Les Hamilton was elected on to the council for North Portslade, and even though he was a Labour man he was chosen as mayor by the Tory majority. Later, when Labour took over the council, Les Hamilton became its last mayor before the merger with Brighton in 1997. He also served for

many years on East Sussex County Council and became its chairman. He was in addition a magistrate at Hove. Known for his quick wit and easy manner, Les Hamilton was a popular man known for a commonsense approach to problems. His son, also Les, is a member of the city council.

Portslade.

808 Dennis Trident – carried name Rudyard Kipling from delivery in April 1999, then renamed Les Hamilton in May 2002. Swapped with 869 (right), originally on METRO Line 1, then METRO Line 7 from April 2004.

870 GILBERT HARDING

Once dubbed the rudest man in Britain, Gilbert Harding had a cutting tongue and was not afraid to use it. He was the first major radio and TV personality in Britain and was a most unlikely choice. After unsuccessful careers as a teacher and a policeman, Harding came to broadcasting almost by accident during the second world war. His gruff manner proved appealing to listeners, and he hosted the radio panel game *Twenty Questions* for many years. He also appeared on TV in *What's My Line?*

Harding had a home in the Montpelier area of Brighton for many years and was an instantly recognisable personality in the town. He would often visit the Theatre Royal, and was always prepared to supply an astringent quote for the local papers. Harding revealed a softer side to his nature shortly before his death when he broke down in tears during a *Face to Face* interview with John Freeman on the subject of his relationship with his mother. He died in 1960 aged only 53 after collapsing with a heart attack on the steps of Broadcasting House in London.

870 Dennis Trident – carried name since delivery in April 2002.

627 PATRICIA HARDING

This well known figure in the world of music was for 51 years a member of Brighton Orpheus Choir. She joined in 1948 after becoming head of music at Varndean Grammar School for Girls. Patricia Harding retired from the school in 1980 after 32 years, and was eventually made an MBE.

The choir prospered under her direction and quickly increased in size. Members were encouraged to venture into work of all kinds, even if they proved difficult. A full house of more than 500 enjoyed her last concert in 1999 – a performance of Haydn's *Creation* in All Saints church, Hove. She died the following year.

Brighton Orpheus Choir logo.

627 Scania Omnidekka – carried name since delivery in February 2004 on METRO Line 1.

PATRICIA HARDING

Brighton&Hove

627

The story of Phoebe Hessel is one of the most remarkable in the whole of Brighton's turbulent history. Born in Limehouse in 1713, she wanted to join the Army and had to pretend to be a man in order to do so. Her brave deceit was not found out for many years. Phoebe was at that time married to a soldier, William Golding, and had enlisted to be with him when he served in the West Indies. When her husband was wounded and invalided out, Phoebe revealed her sex to the commanding officer and was discharged. Golding died and Phoebe married William Hessel after moving to Brighton.

Phoebe's gravestone.

He died when she was 80, but she was not finished yet. She received three guineas from the parish, with which she bought a donkey and hawked fish and other goods. She became a character in Brighton, and in 1800, when she was 87, she was selling gingerbread and apples in the Old Steine. In 1808 the Prince Regent gave her a pension of half a guinea a week – not a bad sum in those days. Blind and aged, she attended his coronation celebrations in 1821 but died in December of the same year. She had lived to the remarkable age of 108 and was buried in the churchyard of St Nicholas in Dyke Road.

807 Dennis Trident – carried name since delivery in April 1999. Name was spelt as Hessell (*above right*) until corrected in May 2001. Originally on METRO Line 1, then METRO Line 7 from April 2004.

872 CAPTAIN HENRY HILL

Members of Brighton Council were an imposing bunch during Victorian times, and Captain Henry Hill was among their number. He lived in a fine house at Marine Parade from 1865 until 1882 and was a councillor for many years. Hill chaired the Fine Arts sub committee and was largely responsible for developing the art gallery in Church Street. His own collection of 400 pictures has been split among galleries throughout the world. His paintings included a Whistler, a Monet and seven works by Degas. Brighton's art collection is one of the best in the province but sadly much of it has to be kept in store because of a lack of display space. Hill would almost certainly have left his collection to Brighton, but there was an argument between him and the corporation which led to the pictures being auctioned at Christie's instead.

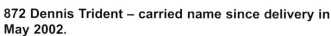

872 Dennis Trident – carried name since delivery in May 2002.

873 SIR ROWLAND HILL

The inventor of the penny post lived at Hanover Crescent in Brighton in the 1840s. Hill, who was born in 1795, became a teacher. Introducing a system of self-government in his school in Birmingham, he argued that moral influence of the highest kind should be the chief power in school discipline.

Hill retired from teaching in 1833 and went on to invent a rotary printing press, but his fame derives chiefly from evolving a system of pre-paid penny postage which was adopted in 1839. He was also the chairman of the London & Brighton Railway and a director of the London, Brighton & South Coast Railway. Hill became secretary to the Post Office in 1854 and retired 10 years later. He was knighted in 1860 and died in 1879.

A penny black.

873 Dennis Trident – carried name since delivery in April 2002.

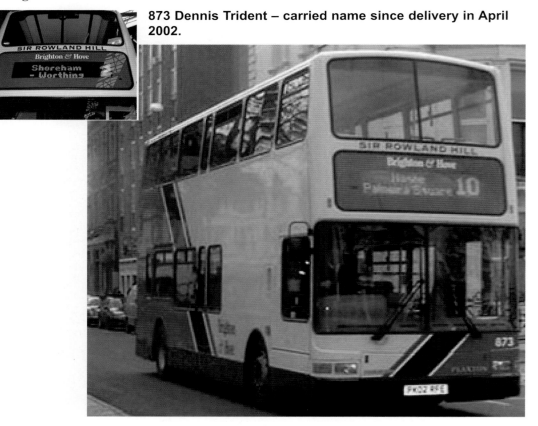

830 SIR JACK HOBBS

There have ben few, in any, finer batsmen than Hobbs, and none who was more modest about his achievements. During a career which was interrupted by the first world war, Hobbs scored more first class runs and centuries than anyone else. He opened the batting for Surrey and for England, where his famous partner was Herbert Sutcliffe. He scored a hundred of his centuries after reaching an age when most cricketers had retired – 40. Hobbs ran a sports shop in London

after giving up the game. Later he came to live in Hove and is buried in the cemetery off the Old Shoreham Road. There is a plaque on a house in Palmeira Avenue.

Hobbs and Sutclffe taking the field for England.

830 Dennis Trident – carried name since delivery in March 2000. Originally on METRO Line 1, then METRO Line 7 from April 2004.

628 DENNIS HOBDEN

Born in Robert Street, Dennis Hobden never left Brighton, and he became one of its best known sons. He started work in the Post Office and was a leading light in its union. He also became prominent in local politics and was elected on to the old Brighton Council. He stood in 1964 for the parliamentary seat of Kemp Town which had been Tory since being formed in 1950. In a famous contest he beat the Tory MP David James by seven votes after seven counts, helping to give Harold Wilson's Labour party a narrow majority. Many people claimed to be among those seven.

Hobden proved to be a hard working, controversial MP, winning again by a narrow majority in 1966. But in 1970 he lost to Andrew Bowden and never regained the seat. His council career continued

and he was elected mayor by the then Tory authority. He chaired committees when Labour took control in 1986. A well-liked man with an impish sense of humour and excellent oratory, Hobden had unusual interests for a Labour MP, including spiritualism and being a freemason. He died in 1995.

Left: The elegant Georgian facades of Kemp Town.

628 Scania Omnidekka – carried name since delivery in March 2004 on METRO Line 1.

607 GEORGE HOLE

Neighbours of George Hole in Sanyhils Avenue, Patcham, thought they were living next door to a secret agent. But the 12ft-long object pointing towards the skies was not a secret weapon. It was a telescope, and Mr Hole was an amateur astronomer a cut above the average. Even today his ground-breaking pictures of the moon are on display at Foredown Tower in Portslade.

Mr Hole manufactured telescopes and special lenses. His largest telescope was used during the 50th transmission of *The Sky at Night* on BBC TV. In 1961 the BBC asked if they could use his telescope when the Russians attempted a moon landing. Over the years many pictures of space were broadcast from the garden of his home, culminating in those of the Apollo moon landing in 1969. Mr Hole's company was

based in Middle Road, Brighton, and Patrick Moore was among the directors. In 1967 the Royal Greenwich Observatory approached him to make a copy of the world's first reflecting telescope designed by Sir Isaac Newton, and this was presented to the Queen. Mr Hole, who had three children, died in 1986 aged 73.

The waxing gibbous moon.

607 Scania Omnidekka – carried name since delivery in July 2003.

831 SIR JOHN HOWARD

For a brief period in the 1890s Brighton had three piers – the old Chain Pier crumbling into the sea, the beautiful West Pier and the new Palace Pier under construction. The man behind the new pier, which was eventually to become one of the most popular leisure attractions in the country, was Sir John Howard. Work actually started on the pier in 1891, but progress was slow and the storm that destroyed the Chain Pier in 1896 brought wreckage into the construction and damaged it. The Brighton Marine Palace and Pier Company, which had been financing the new pier, almost fell into liquidation, but Sir John Howard formed a new company to buy the structure. He completed the pier and opened it in 1899. Initially all it had was an illuminated archway and some kiosks, but it proved a great success and new buildings quickly followed. The pier, bought by the Noble Organisation in 1984 (and later rechristened Brighton Pier), now has about four million visitors a year. Sir John also formed the Howard Convalescent Home in Kemp Town and built a wing of the Royal Sussex County Hospital in Eastern Road.

The present owners have restyled the attraction Brighton Pier.

831 Dennis Trident – carried name since delivery in March 2000 on METRO Line 49.

629 GEORGE HUMPHREY

Although well known as a councillor, George Humphrey also had an interest in mental health and pioneered many reforms, and he always put those achievements above those of his long career on Brighton Council. He was leader of the Labour group in the years before the party gained control in 1986. Humphrey represented Stanmer ward in the north of the town: he was eventually made an honorary alderman. He was a member of the General Workers' union and one of the officials he worked with, John Edmonds, became the general secretary. Many councillors in Brighton regarded him as their mentor, including future mayors David

Preston Park, which George Humphrey helped protect through the Friends.

Lepper (who became MP for Pavilion) and Pat Hawkes. George Humphrey and his wife Babs later moved to the Preston Park area and celebrated their diamond wedding anniversary there. He won improvements for leaseholders in a test case involving residents in his own flats. Humphrey also started the Friends of Preston Park, which achieved many improvements in the area. He died at the age of 84.

629 Scania Omnidekka – carried name since delivery in February 2004 on METRO Line 1.

The former editor of the *Daily Express* and *News of the World* and Radio 2 presenter lived in Hove for many years and wrote for the *Argus*.

Above: Do they mean me? Derek Jameson with 'his' bus.

Right: One of his *Argus* columns.

11 Dennis Dart – carried name from December 2001. Was originally on bus No. 14 on METRO Line 7 from September 1999, then bus repainted red from July 2000 and moved to bus No. 11 until April 2004, when bus was sold.

812 THOMAS KEMP

An extraordinarily powerful figure, Thomas Kemp gave his name to the eastern side of Brighton which is known as Kemp Town. His greatest achievements were the enormous and splendid Regency buildings that grace Sussex Square and Lewes Crescent. It was his farmhouse, rented by the Prince of Wales, that was later demolished to make way for the Royal Pavilion. Kemp became MP for Lewes, winning the former seat of his father, but in 1816 he resigned and founded a religious sect. He built his own chapel in Ship Street and preached there for six years. Soon after he moved to a house called The Temple in Montpelier Road, now part of Brighton & Hove High School. He resumed his political career as MP for Arundel before returning to Lewes. Lord of the Manor, a magistrate and a town commissioner, he gave away large tracts of land for public buildings such as hospitals. Eventually he ran into financial difficulties and had to leave the country. He died in Paris in 1844, but there is a tablet to his memory in St Nicholas church.

812 Dennis Trident – carried name since delivery in April 1999. Originally on METRO Line 1, then repainted into new livery in February 2004. On METRO Line 7 from April 2004.

608 ALBERT KETÈLBEY

The first millionaire composer was born in Birmingham in 1875. Albert Ketèlbey showed a talent for music from a young age and was composing pieces by the time he reached his teens. He went to Trinity College of Music and beat Gustav Holst in a scholarship competition. Ketèlbey achieved critical success for his choral and chamber music, but his greatest success was in more popular pieces which brought him fame and money – among them *Bells Across the Meadow*, *In a Persian Market*, *In a Chinese Temple* and *In a Monastery Garden*. He often chose exotic subjects which appealed strongly to sentimental audiences.

His work was popular with theatre audiences, and in the 1920s he became leader of the West Pier orchestra in Brighton. His music is now rather out of fashion but was at one time thought worthy of comparison with that of Strauss and Lehar.

608 Scania Omnidekka – carried name since delivery in June 2003.

869 RUDYARD KIPLING

Before the days of radio and TV well-known writers often enjoyed great popularity. In late Victorian times there were few more popular than Rudyard Kipling, who came to live in Rottingdean in 1897. Kipling moved to The Elms to be near his aunt Georgina, wife of the painter Sir Edward Burne-Jones, who lived at North End House. While living at The Elms, just off the Green, Kipling wrote some of his most famous works, including *Kim, Stalky and Co* and many of the *Just So*

The Elms at Rottingdean.

stories. While there he also wrote the poems *Recessional* and *Sussex*, possibly the finest ever written about the county.

Kipling didn't enjoy being gawped at by curious members of the public, some of whom arrived in the village by coach especially to see him. In 1903 he moved to Bateman's, in the then remote village of Burwash, East Sussex, and he remained there until his death in 1936. (The house is owned by the National Trust, is open to the public during the summer and has many mementoes of the writer in his book-lined study.)

There is a permanent exhibition about Kipling in Rottingdean at the Grange museum. Developers sought to build on part of the large garden at The Elms, but in 1986 villagers saved it by buying the land and passing it on to Brighton Council to manage as the Kipling Garden.

869 Dennis Trident – delivered in April 2002. Originally named Les Hamilton; renamed in May 2002, swapping with 808.

Originally displayed on bus 808.

832 DAVID LAND

The chief claim to fame of the impresario David Land was taking a risk on the young song-writing team of Tim Rice and Andrew Lloyd Webber. *Jesus Christ Superstar* and *Evita* proved sure-fire successes, making the reputation of the two men and a fortune for Mr Land. It was when he heard in 1984 that two councillors were thinking of buying the Theatre Royal in New Road, Brighton, that David Land took another gamble. He decided to buy the grand old theatre himself, and ran it with panache for more than a decade. His connections brought many

Receiving an honorary degree at Sussex University.

stars to the city, and top shows (including *Evita*) were staged here. Mr Land was said to have subsidised the theatre to the tune of £400,000 a year. It was an act of great generosity and it gave him great pleasure. After his death his family ran the theatre for a while, but it was eventually sold to the Ambassador group, which has continued to bring top class theatre to the Sussex coast.

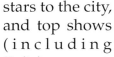

832 Dennis Trident – carried name since delivery in March 2000 on METRO Line 49.

851 THE LAWRENCE SISTERS

Probably the most famous girls' school in Britain, Roedean was founded in 1885 by three sisters, Dorothy, Millicent and Penelope Lawrence. It was based in Lewes Crescent, had 10 girls and was so modest that it didn't even have a name. The school expanded to include other addresses in Kemp Town before moving to Sussex Square, where it was known as Wimbledon House School. Its grand buildings overlooking the sea at Roedean were designed by Sir John Simpson on land owned by the Marquess of Abergavenny. Work started on the imposing structure in 1897 and was finished two years later. The school expanded steadily after that and has added many other buildings. It has one of the best academic records in the country.

851 Dennis Trident – carried name since delivery in March 2001 on METRO Line 5.

630 HARRY LEADER

Harry Leader was one of the best known British bandleaders and songwriters before and after the last war. Born in London, the son of a Russian Army trumpeter, he taught himself how to play alto sax and clarinet. His professional career began at the Regent Ballroom in Brighton, and he returned there as resident bandleader between 1959 and 1963. Leader wrote more than 350 songs, many of them with his wife Rona, and sold millions of records. His career spanned three generations of jazz and swing, extending from the dance band days to the Beatles. His signature tune was Music Maestro Please, but the best known song he wrote was Little Man You've Had a Busy

Day. Leader and his band often appeared on BBC radio, particularly *Music While You Work*. He discovered Matt Monro, the bus driver who became an internationally famous singing star. Leader completed his life story on cassette just before his death in Brighton in 1987, aged 73.

Left: Michael Leader, Harry's son, helped launch his father's bus. Michael is regularly seen in Eastenders driving his milk-float in Albert Square.

630 Scania Omnidekka – carried name since delivery in March 2004 on METRO Line 1.

631 BOBBY LEE

Born in Canada, Bobby Lee became a superstar in Brighton, where he played ice hockey both before and after the Second World War. In 1936 he joined the Brighton Tigers, who played at the Sports Stadium in West Street, but the following season he played in London. During the war he went back to Canada where he joined the Services. Returning to England, he found his London side not operating and so he went back to Brighton. In the 1946/47 season he was player-coach for the Tigers and they won the National League, the National Tournament and the Autumn Cup. Lee and two colleagues set a record for the most points scored in one season by a line in Britain – more than 200. He also became the first player to reach the 400-goal mark in British ice hockey. The Tigers also gained honours the following season and in 1950/51. Lee reached a career total of 472 goals before he retired in 1954. After that he became a publican, running the Mile Oak Inn and the Windmill at Southwick. He died in 1974 aged 63.

631 Scania Omnidekka – carried name since delivery in March 2004 on METRO Line 1.

874 EDWARD LOWTHER

Many councillors in Victorian times had specialities on the authority, and Edward Lowther's chief preoccupation was water. It was vital to have a pure supply in Brighton because water, then as now, had to be pumped from under the Downs. Lowther joined the council in 1884 and was on the board of the Waterworks Committee. The council ran its own water undertaking until about 1973. One of the main pumping engines at the Falmer works was named after him, and there is also a Lowther Road in Brighton.

Born in Nothumberland, he retained his north country accent despite living most of his life in the south. He worked in colleries and graduated to a company secretary before setting up as a coal merchant in Brighton. Lowther had a fall when visiting an electricity works, and this hastened his death in 1912. A plaque was installed in his memory at the Methodist church in London Road.

Lowther Road – named after the man who had a preoccupation with water.

874 Dennis Trident – carried name since delivery in April 2002.

632 IDA LUPINO

A member of the famous theatrical family, she is believed to have been born in 1914 although there was always doubt about her exact age. The Lupinos were known as the Royal Family of Greasepaint, and her father Stanley was a well-known writer of musical comedies. Both her parents went to work in America when she was seven, leaving Ida at a school in Norman Road, Hove, and to be looked after by relatives in the holidays. She appeared in local shows at the Hippodrome in Brighton and at Hove Town Hall. She also wrote a play while at school, produced it and took a leading role. Her parents later returned and encouraged her theatrical activities, even building a small theatre for her and her sisters.

Ida's first film was called *The Love Race*, and she spent some tme in Hollywood. She also appeared in *Thank Your Lucky Stars* and *The Light That*

Failed, which made her a star. Later she appeared in *High Sierra*, *The Hard Way*, *Road House* and *Beware My Lovely*, before achieving more success in *The Big Knife*. Ida Lupino became a director in 1949 when that was unusual for a woman. She also produced some of her films and made many dramas for TV. She married and divorced three times before her death in 1995, when she was probably over 80. There is a plaque on the former school in Norman Road, but her films are her best memorial.

632 Scania Omnidekka – carried name since delivery in February 2004 on METRO Line 1.

15 DES LYNAM

Our best known BBC and ITV sports commentator attended Varndean school, worked locally as an insurance agent and launched his broadcasting career at BBC Radio Brighton in the late 1960s. He was voted Sports Presenter of the Year no fewer than five times.

15 Dennis Dart – carried name from September 1999 on METRO Line 7 until January 2001 when the bus was repainted into new livery.

855 SAKE DEAN MAHOMED

Brighton was full of baths in the late eighteenth century when it had become the Queen of Watering Places. None was more remarkable than the vapouring and shampooing bath opened by Sake Dean Mahomed on the site of the present Queen's Hotel. Dating from 1786, it was more like a Turkish bath and a room for massage, which was then called shampooing. This was done by an attendant through flannel sleeves in a tent cover. Mahomed was a dab hand at promoting his baths, and the service became extremely popular. He was appointed shampooing surgeon to George IV, and William IV continued the appointment. He was a good advertisment for his own

practices as he lived to be 102, dying in 1851. Mahomed is buried in St Nicholas churchyard. The baths were eventually taken over by Charles Brill and were named after him.

855 Dennis Trident – carried name since delivery in March 2001. First named 'Deen' in error: changed to Sake Dean Mahomed in December 2002 on METRO Line 5.

852 TREVOR MANN

Trevor Mann was a childen's doctor whose skill saved the lives of many babies in Brighton. He founded a special babycare unit at the Royal Sussex County Hospital in Brighton. The unit is still there and is named after him. It caters for around 450 premature babies every year. Dr Mann set up the unit, initially at the Royal Alexandra Hospital for Sick Children in Dyke Road, in 1970. He did so after reading an article in the medical journal the *Lancet* about new artificial breathing techniques being used to treat young babies with a low birth weight. The unit has become one of the foremost centres for treating these babies and has dramatically lowered the death rate. Dr Mann died from cancer in 1996.

852 Dennis Trident – carried name since delivery in March 2001 on METRO Line 5.

609 GIDEON MANTELL

No one suspected the existence of dinosaurs until Mary Ann, the wife of Dr Gideon Mantell, decided to go with him to see a patient. While the doctor did his work she went for a walk in the country and saw something shining in a pile of stones left for road-mending. She found that it was a rock containing large and unfamiliar fossil teeth, and she showed it to her husband, who was intrigued. Dr Mantell, based in Lewes, had collected fossils since boyhood. He found that they had come from a quarry in a forest near Cuckfield. Experts thought they were of fairly recent origin, but Mantell persisted until he found that they were similar to those of iguanas – although the teeth of Mantell's creature were 10 times bigger. He calculated that they had belonged to an animal 40ft long, which he called an iguanadon. His discovery caused a stir a few years later when an almost complete iguanadon was found in a quarry near Maidstone. Mantell moved to the Old Steine in Brighton in 1833 and opened his collection of fossils to the public, attracting thousands of visitors. Mary got fed up with his obsession and returned to Lewes. Mantell moved to London and died in 1852, aged 62. People have been fascinated by dinosaurs ever since.

Iguanadon.

**609 Scania Omnidekka –
carried name since delivery
in June 2003.**

853 WILLIAM MARSH

Electric trams run by Brighton Corporation started running in 1901 – an early example of municipal enterprise. Four years later William Marsh was appointed general manager and engineer, and he became something of a local legend. Under his guidance the tram system of nearly 10 miles was used to run regular, efficient and cheap public transport. Sadly in 1939 the council decided to scrap the system because of its lack of flexibility, replacing it with trolleybuses. By this time the trams had run more than

40 million miles and carried more than 6,000 passengers. They also made a profit for the town. Marsh remained at the helm until the end, retiring when the trams disappeared.

853 Dennis Trident – carried name since delivery in March 2001 on METRO Line 5.

Born in Brighton in 1858, he grew up to become one of the most successful barristers of his day. F.E. Smith (later the Earl of Birkenhead), Rufus Isaacs (later the Marquess of Reading) and Edward (later Sir Edward) Carson were all practising at the same time, and they formed a spectacular quartet of legal brilliance, very often opposing one another. Marshall-Hall was probably the most dramatic of them in court. He achieved such a good reputation acting on behalf of notorious alleged murderers that he was known as The Great Defender. Appointed King's Counsel, he built up a flourishing and successful law practice and entered parliament as a Unionist, but he suffered a decline in his fortunes in later life. There is a plaque to him on his house in the Old Steine. Marshall-Hall was a model for many later criminal barristers, notably Lord Birkett.

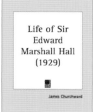

Life of Sir
Edward
Marshall Hall
(1929)

James Churchward

871 Dennis Trident – carried name since delivery in April 2002. Originally named Sir Edward Hall, and renamed in May 2002.

610 ALAN MELVILLE

Largely forgotten now, Alan Melville was a talented all-round entertainer who was best known in the first 30 years after the last war.

He was a revue author, playwright and lyricist during the 1940s and 1950s, with successes such as *Sweet and Low*. Melville went on to write *Castle in the Air*, which was a smash hit, and produced the script for *Spring in Park Lane*. He moved to Brighton in 1951 and stayed there until his death in 1983 aged 73. By then he had become a TV and radio personality, at his best in whimsical, half-hour comedy shows. Melville lived in Clifton Terrace before moving to Victoria Street, from which address he took an active part in local affairs.

610 Scania Omnidekka – carried name since delivery in June 2003.

833 ANDREW MELVILLE

For many years the Grand in North Road was the most popular theatre in Brighton, and one reason for this was the ownership of Andrew Melville. A member of a theatrical family whose connections with the stage went back to 1760, Melville was born in 1884 and had two brothers. They were known as The Three Musketeers of Melodrama. He managed the Grand between 1922 and 1931, producing pantomimes there after that date. Melville also wrote melodramas,

including *Dracula* and *Jack the Ripper*.

He took the leading role in *Sweeny Todd*, which brought him much praise and many fan letters. He also played Bill Sykes in *Oliver Twist* to great effect. Once, when musicians went on strike, he employed street players to ensure that the show would go on. In 1928, after marrying the nurse who had cared for his dying wife, Melville bought a big house called Whychcote in South Street, Portslade. He became chairman of Portslade council in 1933 but was less successful in his efforts to become a councillor in Brighton. Melville died of heart failure aged 54. Although he made a lot of money, he was generous, too, and his widow was forced to move to a smaller house in Shoreham after his death.

833 Dennis Trident– carried name since delivery in March 2000 on METRO Line 49.

834 HERBERT MENGES

Born in 1902, Menges was an infant prodigy, playing the violin from the age of three. His mother formed the Brighton Symphonic Players, and when Menges conducted them in 1925 at Hove Town Hall this is generally reckoned to have marked the foundation of the Brighton Philharmonic Orchestra. Menges became musical director from then until his death in 1972, and he is well remembered today. He also became musical director of the Royalty Theatre in London and founded the London Rehearsal Orchestra in 1931 to help young musicians learn difficult pieces. Menges directed music at the Old Vic in London and conducted many other national orchestras, including the Royal Philharmonic. Rubinstein, Dame Myra Hess and Solomon were among the many musicians who recognised his talent as a conductor. A memorial to him in the Dome records that he conducted 326 concerts there while musical director of the Phil. It adds: 'He founded a tradition which is his permanent memorial.'

834 Dennis Trident – carried name since delivery in March 2000 on METRO Line 49.

819 MAX MILLER

Born Thomas Sargent in a Brighton back street in 1895, the young comedian changed his name to Max Miller and topped the bill in music halls for the best part of half a century. He joined Billy Smart's circus as a boy and went solo during the First World War, when people began to call him the Cheeky Chappie. Miller achieved national, even international, fame yet never lost his Brighton roots. He lived in or near the town for most of his life and had a clause  built into his London contracts that he should be able to catch the last train back to the coast.

Miller was the master of the double entendre and innuendo. He was never directly lewd, although his near-the-knuckle humour got him into trouble with the BBC. He made some films and appeared frequently on the radio, but he was at his best with a live audience who could see his larger-than-life clothes and appreciate his rapport with people. Miller was reputed to be mean and was said never to have paid for a drink when with fans, but he gave generously to charities, especially those connected with the blind. His later years were spend in Camelford Street, Kemp Town, and he died in 1963. Neither his patter nor his repertoire of jokes has been forgotten by fans, and a statue is to be erected in Brighton in his memory.

819 Dennis Trident convertible open-topper – carried name since delivery in May 1999. Changed to Micky Adams–Bobby Zamora during May 2001, then back to Max Miller.

854 DAVID MOCATTA

The orginal facade of Brighton Station was designed by David Mocatta. Unfortunately it was largely hidden by ugly later additions which did nothing for the listed building. Mocatta's design was in the Italianate style and included a long roof over the platforms. It also had a handsome clock, recently restored. They all date from 1841. Mocatta also designed the impressive classical pavilions and balustrades on John Rastrick's Ouse Valley viaduct at Balcombe. A pupil of Sir John Soane, the designer of the Bank of England,Mocatta is reputed to have played a significant part in that enterprise. He was architect to the London, Brighton & South Coast Railway, but little of his work now remains apart from the station, the Grade II listed facade of the now disused synagogue in Devonshire Place and some Italianate houses in Osborne Villas.

854 Dennis Trident – carried name since delivery in March 2001 on METRO Line 5.

773 SOUTHERN FM'S MOODY

Southern FM's Moody was one of two successful bidders when the bus company auctioned names on the front of a bus at the *Argus* Appeal in 2001 – raising more than £5,000 for charity. Moody worked on the radio station's breakfast show.

773 Scania Cityzen – carried name from October 2001 until September 2002.

A s director of the Royal Pavilion in the years after the Second World War, Dr Musgrave had the unenviable job of rescuing the palace from wartime

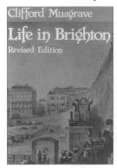

disrepair. But he did much more than that. He persuaded Brighton Council, which owned it, to restore the Pavilion to its original splendour. Each summer he presided over the Regency Exhibition, during which original furniture which had gone elsewhere was lent to the palace. In the end it was returned for year-round display, and Musgrave managed to up the number of visits to almost half a million a year.

He also performed a fine service for Brighton and Hove in 1945 when he became a founder member of the Regency Society, which has done great conservation work ever since. But his most lasting achievement was to have written a seminal book on the town he loved called *Life in Brighton*. First published in 1970, it gives a loving and learned account of the resort from its earliest days to modern times.

611 Scania Omnidekka – carried name since delivery in June 2003.

811 JOHN NASH

When the Prince Regent wanted to build his palace by the sea, he employed one of the leading architects of the day to create the designs for him. John Nash, who was also responsible for many London buildings, including Regent Street, proved equal to the task. Using Indian influences for the outside design and Chinese for the interior, he created a unique building which has remained the symbol of Brighton.

The Royal Pavilion has been restored many times, and the gardens have been redesigned in accordance with Nash's original plans. However, Nash wasn't thanked for his pains. In 1822 he left under a cloud because of the enormous costs of the building, which had overrun by thousands of pounds.

811 Dennis Trident – carried name since delivery in April 1999. Originally on METRO Line 1, then repainted into new livery in April 2004.

856 DAME ANNA NEAGLE

After the Second World War, Brighton attained a reputation for being a resort where actors liked to live. Many of them took the Brighton Belle electric express to London to arrive in plenty of time for West End performances. Among the most notable of the theatrical set was Dame Anna Neagle, who lived in Lewes Crescent. She enjoyed a long and successful career on stage and screen. Her husband was the well-known film director Herbert Wilcox.

Born in 1904, Anna Neagle made her first film in 1930 and her last in 1959. She had begun her career as a dancer and appeared on stage in *Stand Up and Sing* with Jack Buchanan. Wilcox, who was in the audience, spotted that she had talent and offered to put her in his films. The couple married in 1943, and he directed films for her for the rest of her career. She specialised in playing heroines such as Florence Nightingale and Odette. She died in 1986.

Dame Anna starred in Nell Gwynne.

856 Dennis Trident – carried name since delivery in March 2001 on METRO Line 5.

763 NICOLA & DECLAN

What a treat to have your name on a bus when you get married! That's what Nicola and Declan thought – and here they are to prove it.

This was a one-off idea that proved to be an expensive option, and it wasn't offered again.

763 Scania Cityzen – carried name for wedding party for a few days in January 2002. Did not operate in normal service.

16 ANNIE NIGHTINGALE

She was the first female disc jockey on BBC radio and received a Lifetime Achievement from the Music Industry and Related Media Organisation in 2001. She lived in Brighton from the 1970s until the 1990s.

16 Dennis Dart – carried name from September 1999 on METRO Line 7 until April 2004 when the bus was sold.

612 RAY NOBLE

The great bandleader was born in Brighton in 1903 and studied at Cambridge before attending the Royal College of Music. His first hit song was *Goodnight Sweetheart*, which he followed with *By the Fireside, I Found You, What More Can I Ask* and *Love is the Sweetest Thing*. He became the first British bandleader to score a success in the USA, and the young Glenn Miller played trombone in the band. During this time Noble wrote *The Very Thought of You, Loved Looked Out* and *The Touch of Your Lips*.

His band broke up in 1936 and he went to Hollywood to star in *The Big Broadcast* with Bing Crosby and Ethel Merman. Later he appeared with Fred Astaire in *Damsel in Distress*. Noble returned to England in 1938 to appear in variety, but he went back to America shortly afterwards to play musical and comedy roles on the Burns and Allen show. He continued his radio career after the war and retired to Santa Barbara, also spending time in Jersey. He died in 1978 aged 75. He will be best remembered for the songs he composed and for his band, especially the numbers Al Bowlly sang.

612 Scania Omnidekka – carried name since delivery in June 2003.

817 LORD OLIVIER

The greatest actor of his day lived at Royal Crescent in Brighton for many years in the Sixties and Seventies. He had two houses knocked together in this fashionable seafront street, but resented criticism when he applied, perfectly legally, for a conservation grant. Olivier's best known battle in Brighton was in 1972 when he fought to save kippers on the breakfast menu of the Brighton Belle express train to London. He won the battle but lost the war: the kippers remained, but the train itself was axed later that year. Eventually Olivier and his wife, Joan Plowright, moved to the country and lived near Steyning.

Olivier achieved fame for a wide variety of roles on stage and screen, ranging from Shakespearean heroes to Archie Rice in John Osborne's *The Entertainer*.

817 Dennis Trident – carried name since delivery in May 1999. First named Lord Lawrence Olivier in error during July 1999, then changed to Lord Olivier. Originally on METRO Line 1, repainted into new livery from March 2004 and then into new METRO Line 1 livery from April 2004.

835 CECIL PASHLEY

Shoreham Airport was opened in 1910 and is one of the oldest in the country. Much of its early success was owed to aviation pioneers such as Cecil Pashley, who had been attracted to the Brighton area. In 1911 Cecil and his brother Eric founded the Southern Aero Club based at Shoreham, two years after he had taught himself to fly. He bought a cross-Channel Bleriot monoplane when it was still a curiosity. During the First World War he was a test pilot and instructor for the Royal Naval Air Service.

He taught many fighter pilots, including Mick Mannock, born in Brighton, who shot down more aircraft than any other British pilot. Pashley was nicknamed the Grand Old Man of Aviation in his later years. He served in the RAF during the Second World War and spent more than 3000 hours as an instructor teaching pilots in Britain, Canada and parts of Africa. He reopened the flying club at Shoreham after the war and was awarded the MBE. It was reckoned that he taught more people how to fly than any

Cecil Pashley at Shoreham Airport.

other pilot, clocking up 20,000 hours. His wife Vera, who lived to be over a hundred, helped him run the club. He died in 1969 aged 77 and is buried in Mill Lane cemetery. A road at Shoreham Airport is named after him.

835 Dennis Trident – carried name since delivery in March 2000 on METRO Line 49.

836 SIR ARTHUR PEARSON

St Dunstan's is one of the most famous institutions in Brighton, and much of that is due to Sir Arthur Pearson. In 1915, at Bayswater Road in London, he founded the centre for men and women who had been blinded in conflict. Called the Blind Soldiers and Sailors Hostel, it was so successful that it soon moved to a villa at Regent's Park called St Dunstan's, and the name stuck: the building is now the home of the US ambassador. By the end of the war nearly 2,000 war-blinded men were being trained for work in civvy street. A convalescent home was opened at this

The St Dunstan's building at Ovingdean.

time in St George's Road, Brighton, and in 1957 the building was renamed Pearson House. Although it was extensively renovated in 1973, the historic facade, which dated from 1847, was preserved. It is now owned by the major hospital trust in Brighton. The yellow brick building at Ovingdean was built just before the Second World War. Its foundation stone was laid in 1937 by Lady Pearson, Sir Arthur's widow.

836 Dennis Trident – carried name since delivery in April 2000 on METRO Line 49.

866 PRINCE PHILIP

To celebrate the Queen's golden jubilee two buses were painted in a gold livery in 2002.

866 Dennis Trident – carried name from April 2002 until January 2003, when bus renamed Bride & Groom.

837 MARGARET POWELL

A delightful character, Margaret Powell achieved fame late in life when she found she had a natural talent as a raconteur and writer. Born in 1907, she was the eldest daughter in a family of seven, and she had to look after some of her siblings. Because her parents couldn't afford to keep her at school to achieve her wish of being a teacher, she had to go into domestic service. She did this for 10 years before marrying a milkman called Albert. They had three

sons. When they had grown up, she brushed up her education and went to night school to take O and A levels. She was discovered in 1966 when the BBC took her from her evening class group to talk about her life in service. A publisher who was listening was impressed and asked if she wanted to write a book. The result was the best seller *Below Stairs*, and she went on to write 17 other books in similar vein, showing a sharp eye for detail and comedy.

Her infectious laugh became well known on radio and TV, and she delighted in her celebrity. Margaret Powell fought breast cancer for many years while going through the agony of watching her oldest son, David, die from a brain tumour. She died in 1984. She had lived in Old Shoreham Road, Hove, where a blue plaque has been erected in her memory.

837 Dennis Trident – carried name since delivery in April 2000 on METRO Line 49.

813 SIR HARRY PRESTON

Brighton was in the doldrums early last century when the most unlikely figure came along to help save her. Sir Harry Preston ran both the Royal York and Royal Albion Hotels, next door to each other in the Old Steine. He had arrived in Brighton in 1900 from Bournemouth, where he had already been a successful hotelier. Preston put his money and a huge amount of effort into rescuing the flagging fortune of his two hotels and of the resort as a whole. When the *Daily Mail* published an unflattering piece about the town, Preston went to London and saw the editor – a much more favourable article appeared the following day and did a lot to improve Brighton's reputation.

The Royal Albion Hotel.

Preston attracted the top writers, sportsmen and other celebrities of the day to stay with him. Arnold Bennett wrote his novel *Clayhanger* while staying in Brighton and boxers who appeared at his annual charity shows in the Dome included Jack Dempsey, Georges Carpentier, Bombadier Billy Wells, Boy McCormack and Billy Wilde. He also helped make Brighton an early centre for motor racing by insisting that Madeira Drive be paved. He was also keenly interested in the early aviation pioneers who operated from Shoreham. A small man with a big personality, Sir Harry Preston was a dominant figure in the resort for 30 years. The Albion remains as a hotel, but the York was used as council offices until being sold in 2003.

813 Dennis Trident – carried name since delivery in April 1999, originally on METRO Line 1 then repainted into new livery from February 2004.

Brighton was already a fashionable place when the future King George IV first set eyes on the town during the late eighteenth century, but he played his part in ensuring that the windswept fishing centre became the Queen of Watering Places. When George made his first visit a salute from the battery in his honour killed the gunner. George bought a farmhouse and asked the architect John Nash to transform it into the most fantastic palace in Europe, and he furnished his Royal Pavilion lavishly. He created two of the most beautiful rooms anywhere in the Music Room and the Banqueting Room. He entertained royally and would sometimes consume as many as 36 courses with his guests. It was small wonder that the slim and handsome young man became an obese and ugly monarch.

George became Regent in 1811 when his father, George III, was declared insane. He was king from 1820 to 1830, but by this time his love affair with Brighton was over, and he spent much more time at Windsor. George finished the Pavilion in 1821 but became fed up with the crowds in Brighton. He made his last visit here in 1828.

803 Dennis Trident – carried name since delivery in March 1999. Originally on METRO Line 1, then METRO Line 7 from April 2004.

875 JOHN RASTRICK

Born in Northumberland in 1780, Rastrick patented a steam engine in 1814 and also built a cast-iron bridge over the Wye at Chepstow. He worked closely with George Stephenson and was one of the judges which

chose the Rocket in celebrated steam trials. Rastrick became chief engineer of the London & Brighton Railway, displaying great boldness in all that he did. Stephenson said that the direct route chosen by the company for the line from London to Brighton was impractical because of the immense engineering feats needed, but Rastrick went ahead with building the long Merstham, Balcombe and Clayton tunnels, the last of them more than a mile long. Rastrick was also responsible for the line to Lewes, which involved a 28-arch viaduct over land at Preston Road in Brighton. He designed the splendid viaduct over the Ouse Valley at Balcombe, with David Mocatta designing the classical pavilions at each end. He is buried in the extra mural cemetery at Brighton, and has a particularly imposing tomb.

Top: The castellated entrance to Rastrick's Clayton tunnel.

Bottom: His impressive tomb.

875 Dennis Trident – carried name since delivery in April 2002.

617 DOUGLAS REEVE

Douglas Reeve showed an interest in music at an early age and gave his first public perfomance as an organist at the old Regent cinema in Queen's Road when he was 15. Born in The Lanes, Brighton, he was discovered in 1934 by BBC staff organist Reginald Foort, who engaged him to play in cinemas as The Wonder Boy Organist. Reeve started playing the famous organ at the Dome in Brighton after he had

been invalided out of the Army. He was a regular at Tuesday Night at the Dome, which ran for all of 1,600 performances and earned a place in the Guinness Book of Records as the longest running variety programme. Reeve made hundreds of broadcasts and many recordings at the Dome and eventually became manager of the building too. Brighton Council made him assistant resort director in

The famous Dome organ.

1977, and he retired two years later. Reeve's theme tune was *Pack Up Your Troubles*, which he adopted during the dark days of the Second World War – he once even carried on playing during an air raid, while on another occasion a bomb landed on the western lawn of the Royal Pavilion during one of his concerts. Reeve lived at Woodingdean, where he had a Wurlitzer and a piano installed in a sound-proofed room. He died in 1999 aged 81.

617 Scania Omnidekka convertible open-topper – carried name since delivery in June 2003.

820 DAME FLORA ROBSON

Dame Flora as Queen Elizabeth I.

Many stage and screen actors and actresses came to live in Brighton after the Second World War. Among them was Dame Flora Robson, doyenne of the British stage and screen for many decades. Never showy or stuck up, Dame Flora was well loved in her adopted town. She lived in Marine Gardens during the Sixties and Seventies when she was still active on the stage. Later she moved to Wykeham Terrace near the Clock Tower and seldom turned down an invitation to open a fete or garden party in aid of charity. Among the many buildings she opened was the pioneering toy library in Whitehawk in 1973. Dame Flora appeared many times at the Theatre Royal, but was more often in long runs in the West End.

820 Dennis Trident convertible open-topper – carried name from delivery in May 1999. Changed to The Albion Team 2001/02 during May 2002, then back to Dame Flora Robson.

804 DR RICHARD RUSSELL

An obscure doctor from Lewes was the unlikely midwife of the modern resort in England by telling his patients to take the seawater cure. He made them both swim in it and drink it – which did them no harm and may even have done them some good. Soon people began to flock to Brighton where the experiments had taken place in the middle of the eighteenth century. He published a paper called A

Dr Russell's Sea Water Cure

Dissertation on the Use of Sea Water in the Affections of the Glands which was the first to claim medicinal qualities for seawater. Russell recommended patients to try the nearest place to Lewes by the sea, which was Brighton. As his fame increased he moved to Brighton, building what was then the largest house there. He died in 1759 and there is a plaque to his memory in South Malling church, Lewes. He is also remembered in a plaque on the Royal Albion Hotel, the site of his seafront house. Echoing Wren's monument at St Paul's, it reads: 'If you seek his monument, look around'.

804 Dennis Trident – carried name since delivery in March 1999. Originally on METRO Line 1, then METRO Line 7 from April 2004.

857 SIR RICHARD SACKVILLE

The Sackville family lived at Hangleton Manor, the oldest secular building in Brighton and Hove, for more than 300 years. Sir Richard was a Sussex MP and a cousin of Ann Boleyn, one of Henry VIII's six wives. He was born in the same year as Ann, and his eldest son, Thomas,

Hangleton Manor.

was born in the year when she was beheaded. Richard Sackville had such a good head for figures that he gained the odd nickname of Fillsack. He was knighted in 1549, and the following year he became Lord Lieutenant of Sussex. His land covered thousands of acres in Sussex, and he also owned land in London between Fleet Street and the Thames: when Thomas succeeded him he became one of the richest men in the country. Sackville Road in Hove is named after the family. The Manor, which fell into disrepair in the 1960s, is now a public house.

857 Dennis Trident – carried name since delivery in April 2001 on METRO Line 5

613 JOHN SAXBY

There is a modest plaque on the west side of Brighton Station to a man of whom most people have never heard. Without the work of John Saxby, however, train travel would be a good deal less safe than it is today. Born in Brighton, Saxby continued to live in the town when he became one of the pioneers, with John Farmer, of railway safety – developing a signalling system whereby trains would be kept on separate routes in order to prevent crashes and derailments. Their firm Saxby and Farmer, formed in 1863, later became the Westinghouse Brake and Signal Company.

A Saxby signalbox.

613 Scania Omnidekka – carried name since delivery in July 2003.

17 LEO SAYER

T he international recording artist was first discovered in Brighton in 1970. Born in Shoreham, he spent his early career in Brighton. Adam Faith was one of his co-managers.

17 Dennis Dart – carried name from September 1999 on METRO Line 7 until April 2004, when the bus was sold.

618 DANNY SHELDON

Many people from Wales came to Brighton during the depression between the wars. Among them were the Sheldons, who produced two sons, Danny and Bill – both of whom entered local politics. While Bill was a Labour man, Danny always supported the Conservative cause, representing King's Cliff ward in Kemp Town. One of his achievements was to oversee the building of the Prince Regent pool at a time when Brighton was seriously short of places for people to swim.

He became the first mayor of the new borough of Brighton after local

A young Mike Cheesman meets Danny Sheldon and Mayoress Lilian on a mayoral visit to Southdown House.

government reorganisation in 1974. With his warm manner and charismatic personality, Sheldon was such a hit that some thought he should have been permanetly first citizen of the town. He cared passionately about his adopted town and wouldn't easily compromise over issues on which he felt strong passions. This led him into political hot water, especially when he was promoting the interests of Brighton with his

usual fervour on the county council. Eventually he was de-selected by the Tories, but he fought as an independent to win his ward on both the borough and county councils. The confrontations took a toll on his health, but he had made his peace with the party by the time he died from cancer in 1982 aged 64.

618 Scania Omnidekka convertible open-topper – carried name since delivery in June 2003.

614 SIR CHARLES AUBREY SMITH

Some Hollywood actors, such as David Niven, have enjoyed cricket, but few cricketers have made it big in films. A notable exception was Sir Charles Aubrey Smith, the son of a doctor who was born in Hove. Smith, who lived in Albany Villas, captained Cambridge University before becoming the captain of Sussex and of England too. His curious bowling action, approaching the crease from an angle, caused him to be known as Round the Corner Smith.

One of the films in which Aubrey Smith played an English gent.

After retiring from sport he became an actor and appeared many times on the London stage. Then he went to Hollywood, where he was much in demand for playing English gentlemen. He kept up his cricketing interests in California and founded Hollywood CC whose members included Niven and Boris Karloff. He made frequent visits to his home town and in 1948 watched a cricket match at the county ground in Hove. Smith is buried in a family vault at St Leonard's church in Hove.

614 Scania Omnidekka – carried name since delivery in July 2003.

858 GEORGE ALBERT SMITH

Hollywood may be the place most associated with the film industry, but Hove is where it all started. Film pioneers were active in the town before 1900, and the most notable of them was George Albert Smith. With his partner, the chemist James Williamson, Smith produced a series of short silent films, often with a comic theme. Many of them were shot in St Ann's Well Garden, then private land, where Smith had a studio. He also recorded great events such as Queen Victoria's diamond jubilee procession in 1897, a tour of India by the Prince of Wales and the funeral procession of Edward VII. Next he invented Kinemacolour, the first practical colour film system ever shown to a paying audience.

The studio in St Ann's Well Garden.

He became disillusioned when he was sued over copyright and retired from film-making to become largely forgotten. But after the Second World War interest in the Hove pioneers revived, and Smith was found to be alive, well and living in Hove. He was invited to the opening of the National Film Theatre in London, and lived until 1959, when he had reached the age of 94.

858 Dennis Trident – delivered in March 2001. Originally named Malcolm Farley during April 2001, then changed name in May 2001, on METRO Line 5.

HENRY SOLOMON

Appointed the first chief constable of Brighton in 1838, Solomon achieved a reputation, like his namesake, for wisdom. In those days all civic offices, including the police, were in Brighton Town Hall in Bartholomews. In 1844 a man called John Lawrence was arrested for stealing a carpet from a shop in St James's Street. He was taken to the town hall, where Solomon tried to question him. Because Lawrence was distressed, he was asked to sit near the fire to calm down. Three other officials were in the room at the time, but they failed to keep a careful watch on him. Suddenly he shot up and smashed Solomon's skull with an iron poker from the fireplace. The chief constable died later and Lawrence was charged with murder. He was tried at Lewes, convicted and hanged outside the county gaol in Horsham.

This tragedy shocked Brighton, which had seen much good in the police chief, who was only 50 years old. Sympathy for Solomon and his large sorrowing family extended far beyond the locality. A public meeting to raise money for the support of the bereaved drew more than a thousand pounds. His memorial stone is in the Jewish cemetery in Florence Place.

633 Scania Omnidekka – carried name since delivery in March 2004 on METRO Line 1.

18 DUSTY SPRINGFIELD

The singer lived with her brother Tom in Wilbury Road, Hove, and formed The Springfields before embarking on a solo recording career.

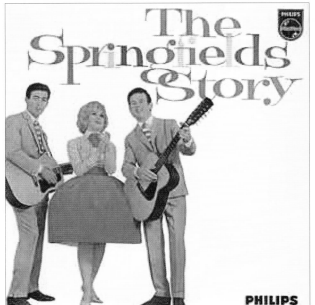

18 Dennis Dart – carried name from September 1999 on METRO Line 7 until April 2004, when the bus was sold.

634 DOROTHY STRINGER

There can be few greater records of service to Brighton than that of Dorothy Stringer. She served 50 years on Brighton Education Committee and never missed a meeting. Miss Stringer was born into public life. Her father was on the council for 34 years, her mother was a member of the Board of Guardians and a cousin became mayor. She was elected to Brighton Council as an independent in 1925 but eventually became a Conservative. By 1964 she was the senior councillor, and she continued to serve until the reorganisation of local government 10 years later.

Miss Stringer chaired the education committee for several years and was honoured when a secondary school in the town was named after her. She became mayor of Brighton in 1952, was awarded the OBE and became a freeman of Brighton. She was also an alderman. As a young woman she sang under the direction of Sir Henry Wood and she was a lifelong member of St Bartholomew's church, singing in the choir. Her record of service can be judged by the fact that in 1969, when in her mid seventies, she served on 40 committees. She died in 1977.

Dorothy Stringer school.

634 Scania Omnidekka – carried name since delivery in March 2004 on METRO Line 1.

Brighton was a big railway centre until the 1960s, and one of its most famous names was William Stroudley, locomotive superintendent of the London, Brighton & South Coast Railway. Succeeding the autocratic John Craven, Stroudley earned the respect of his workers from the moment he was appointed in 1870. He had the idea that every driver should have his name painted in his cab. He rooted out corruption and designed locomotives that became a legend. His Terriers (small tank engines) were so well made that many of them lasted more than 150 years. The oldest is Fenchurch, built in 1872 and now to be seen on the Bluebell Railway. His small Gladstone engines were celebrated as express locomotives and, again, remained in service for many years. He paid great attention to the colour and design of his engines and instilled enormous pride in his work-force. This helped give a mystique to the railway he ran. He died in 1889 from bronchitis after catching a chill at railway trials in France. Thousands of people attended his funeral in Brighton.

838 Dennis Trident – carried name since delivery in April 2000 on METRO Line 49.

802 CAPTAIN NICHOLAS TETTERSELL

Captain Nicholas Tettersell helped the future King Charles II to escape to France when he was on the run. The good ship *Surprise* was used to carry Charles to safety across the English Channel. Later, when Charles had become king, he rewarded the man who had helped preserve his life. Tettersell received a pension of £100 a year for 99 years. With the money Tettersell bought what is now the Old Ship Hotel in King's Road. He became a captain in the Navy before leaving the service. In later years, when High Constable of Brighton, he was noted for his persecution of nonconformists. He is buried in St Nicholas churchyard.

The *Surprise*.

802 Dennis Trident – carried name since delivery in March 1999. Originally on METRO Line 1, then METRO Line 7 from April 2004. Repainted in new livery from June 2004.

839 STANLEY THEOBALD

From humble beginnings Stanley Theobald rose to become one of the most powerful men in Brighton. A surveyor and estate agent, he was rumoured to know the price and value of every house in Brighton and Hove. His firm, George White, brought him wealth, and once his fortune had been made he devoted himself to civic affairs. Joining Brighton Council, he became leader of the ruling Tory

group, and his greatest achievements were in housing. During his long tenure as housing chairman he built more council houses and flats than anyone else: it was appropriate that the tallest council block of them all, Theobald House, was named after him.

Theobald led the way in building the Brighton Centre, the first purpose-built conference venue in Britain, and he chaired the committee which supervised it. He saw early on that the Royal Pavilion needed restoring, and never flinched at the eventual cost of £10 million – the same as building the centre. He was instrumental in ensuring that American Express, Brighton's largest employer,

Theobald House.

established its European headquarters here in 1977. Stanley Theobald became mayor of Brighton, and his son Geoffrey – still a member of Brighton and Hove City Council – later achieved the same honour.

839 Dennis Trident – carried name since delivery in April 2000 on METRO Line 49. Renamed Frank Butterworth during April 2001, then back to Stanley Theobald.

635 ANGELA THIRKELL

Many writers lived in Rottingdean, the most notable of them all being Rudyard Kipling. Their exploits were tenderly recounted by one of their number, Angela Thirkell, in a book called *Three Houses*. First published in 1931, it was about her love for The Grange in Fulham, North End House in Rottingdean and The Elms in the same village. The first two belonged to her grandfather, the painter Sir Edward Burne-Jones, and the third to Kipling. In the book she gives a charming account of a child witnessing the Pre-Raphaelite circle and the writer she called Cousin Ruddy.

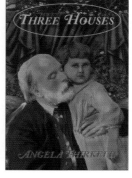

Thirkell was probably best known nationally for her Barsetshire novels, in which she wittily chronicled English country life in the 1930s, 1940s and 1950s. They were based on the novels by Trollope, using his geography and the descendants of some of his characters. Her other work included a biography of the Regency courtesan Harriette Wilson, a collection of children's stories called *The Grateful Sparrow* and *Trooper to the Southern Cross*, a book about a voyage to Australia.

635 Scania Omnidekka – carried name since delivery in February 2004 on METRO Line 1.

Sir Charles Thomas-Stanford and his wife, Lady Ellen, lived at Preston Manor on the outskirts of Brighton. The house was largely built in 1738, but after they moved there in 1905 the Thomas-Stanfords employed architect Charles Reilly to carry out alterations, including a new west wing. They both died in 1932, leaving the lovely eighteenth century

Preston Manor.

manor to Brighton Corporation. Ever since then it has been opened to the public, and is currently shown as in its Edwardian heyday. Sir Charles and Lady Ellen, who were also mayor and mayoress of Brighton, not only left the house to the town but also bequeathed pictures, clocks, furniture, paintings, silver and porcelain.

814 Dennis Trident – carried name since delivery in May 1999. Originally named without the 'Sir', which was added in July 1999. First on METRO Line 1, then repainted in new livery from March 2004.

859 THOMAS TILLING

Born in Hendon in 1825, Tilling developed horse bus services and later switched to motor buses in London. His name became one of the most famous in public transport, and the Tilling Company began operating in Brighton in 1915. It survived until the formation of Brighton, Hove & District Buses, the forerunner of Brighton & Hove Buses, in 1935. Tilling bought a grey mare called Kitty in 1847 and a carriage for £30. He started

a horse bus in 1850. By 1856 he had 70 horses, mostly greys, and by 1897 there were 4,000. He introduced a motor bus in 1904, and the last horse bus ran in 1914, just before the First World War. Other members of the large Tilling family took over running the firm,

but the family connection ended in 1929. The Tilling name disappeared 40 years later with the formation of the National Bus Company.

859 Dennis Trident – carried name since delivery in March 2001 on METRO Line 5.

860 JACK TINKER

One of the best journalists ever to have worked in Brighton, Jack Tinker was theatre critic of the *Evening Argus* in the Sixties. He also undertook a series of star interviews for the paper under the name of Luke Leavis. He became a notable provincial film critic, too, and his work was always both perceptive and beautifully written. Eventually he went to work for the *Daily Mail*, where he achieved national fame. He also occasionally appeared on the stage, thoroughly enjoying himself. Tinker remained living in Brighton, and it was a shock to his many friends when he died from a heart condition in 1995. There's a memorial to him in the western churchyard of St Nicholas in Dyke Road.

860 Dennis Trident – carried name since delivery in March 2001 on METRO Line 5.

861 JOHN VALLANCE

The Vallance family moved from Patcham to Hove in the 1780s and John Vallance built Hove Manor in Hove Street. Born in 1759, he was an early cricketer, and he was in a match at the Level in Brighton in 1790 which was watched by the Prince of Wales. The prince stayed at his home and presented him with an engraved punch bowl which became a family heirloom. John died in 1833. His family, which included several other men called John, was well known for its brewery in West Street, Brighton. Until

recently a ward on Brighton & Hove City Council was named after the family, and roads still bear the name. Vallance is buried in a vault in St Andrew's church, Hove.

St Andrew's church in Hove, where John Vallance is buried.

861 Dennis Trident – carried name since delivery in March 2001 on METRO Line 5.

810 MAGNUS VOLK

This son of a German clockmaker was a great inventor and pioneer in the late nineteenth and early twentieth centuries. He brought electricity early to his own house in Dyke Road and soon had the Royal Pavilion illuminated in the same way. He also brought the first telephone service to Brighton. Volk then built his delightful

Magnus Volk at the wheel.

seafront railway in 1884, the first electric railway in

The Daddy Long Legs.

Britain. It was such a success that it expanded, and it now runs between the Aquarium and Black Rock. More remarkable still, Volk fashioned a railway between Brighton and Rottingdean that ran with its rails in the sea. Nicknamed Daddy Long Legs, the extraordinary contraption made slow but stately progress in the water. It survived the worst the weather could throw at it, but could not bypass new groynes put down by Brighton Corporation to protect the beaches. Volk's own little line was taken over by the council in the late 1930s and it is still council-run today. The inventor himself appeared in public for the last time in 1937 at the opening of a station at Black Rock. He died later the same year, and there is a plaque to his memory on his former home in Dyke Road.

810 Dennis Trident – carried name since delivery in April 1999. Originally on METRO Line 1, then repainted into new livery in January 2004 and on METRO Line 7 from April 2004.

The son of the Rev Henry Wagner, imperious vicar of Brighton, Arthur was perpetual curate of St Paul's church in West Street. Greatly influenced by the High Church ideas of Dr Edward Pusey, Wagner was involved with the controversy over Ango-Catholicism which raged in England during the last half of the nineteenth century. A shy and pious man, he attracted an unusual amount of resentment despite all his good works. He started a community of nuns at Queen Square which was connected with a home for female penitents. One of the residents, Constance Kent, stood trial for murder in 1864. Called as a witness, Wagner refused to reveal details of her confession to the court, and this led to his being attacked and even shot in the streets of Brighton.

St Bartholomew's.

Wagner remained in his post until he died in 1902, having served for 52 years. His chief legacy to the town was the building of five churches in poor areas: St Bartholomew's in Ann Street (one of the finest churches in England), St Martin's, St Mary & St Magdelene, the Church of the Annunciation and the Church of the Resurrection. He also had more than 400 houses built for poor people in the town, mainly in the Roundhill and Islingword Road areas.

876 Dennis Trident – carried name since delivery in April 2002.

615 CHARLIE WEBB

Few men have done more for Brighton & Hove Albion than Charlie Webb, the longest-serving manager. The Irishman was in charge of the team for more than 1,200 games between 1919 and 1947. Webb lived at Frith Road in Hove, where a plaque has been unveiled in his memory. He first played for Albion at West Ham on Christmas Day 1908 and scored on his debut. In a career lasting until 1915 he scored 79 goals in 275 matches. Webb served in the First World War and was captured and imprisoned by the Germans. While he was in captivity he received a letter from Albion's directors offering him the post of manager on his release.

Charlie Webb's benefit year postcard, 1921.

Webb, remembered by colleagues as a gentleman, built a series of fine Albion sides on a shoestring budget. On match days all the gate money was taken to Frith Road and stored in a safe in the larder because the banks weren't open on Saturdays. Webb even sold tickets from the house for cup ties. In 1949 he was honoured with a testimonial match at the Goldstone ground between Arsenal and Portsmouth. He died in 1975, and a tree was planted opposite the ground in his memory.

615 Scania Omnidekka – carried name since delivery in July 2003.

13 ALAN WEEKS

Weeks on the ice.

The famous BBC skating commentating legend lived in the town for many years before his death in 1996. He had a lifetime association with Brighton Tigers, and was president of the club as well as of the Brighton & Hove Entertainment Managers Association. He was honoured by the Sportswriters Association of Great Britain with a lifetime Achievement Award in 1996.

3 Dennis Dart – carried name from February 2002 on METRO Line 7 until April 2004 when the bus was sold.

616 ALLEN WEST

Ever since the 1970s the biggest company in Brighton and Hove has been American Express, which has its European headquarters in Edward Street, but for many years before that it was Allen West, an electrical engineering firm which was based in Lewes Road. It was named after its founder, who started a small business in 1910 making electrical control gear. The firm rapidly expanded, reaching its peak in the 1950s and 1960s when it had more than 3,000 employees. The recessions of the 1980s damaged Allen West as it did all the other engineering firms in Brighton and Hove, but there are still many men and women with fond memories of a company where they spend most of their working lives.

Allen West himself was a sportsman as well as an engineer. He served as a soldier in the Boer War and was present at the relief of Mafeking. After being wounded, he recuperated at Hove. West, who also served in both world wars, was sales engineer as well as managing director for the company, and he travelled extensively in that role. He had a long association with the British Electrical and Allied Manufacturers' Association. West gave up being managing director in 1933 but remained on the board for another 20 years before retiring. He died in 1957 in his 80th year.

616 Scania Omnidekka – carried name since delivery in July 2003. In July 2004 the name was changed to white as a test case to determine whether the names would stand out better on these vehicles.

The resident band in what was the Florida Rooms (at the Aquarium site) during the 1960s, The Who wrote the album *Quadrophenia* which was turned into a cult 'Brighton' film.

19 Dennis Dart – carried name from September 1999 on METRO Line 7 until April 2004 when the bus was sold.

840 AMON WILDS

Born in 1762, Amon Wilds started a building firm in Lewes with his son, Amon Henry Wilds. They moved to Brighton in 1815 and built the Trinity Chapel and the Temple in Montpelier Road for Thomas Read Kemp. In 1822 Wilds went into partnership with the architect Charles Busby, and together they built much of Regency Brighton. The two men built the Kemp Town and Brunswick estates which contain most of the Grade 1 listed buildings in Brighton and Hove. Wilds also built the old Debenhams building in Western Road (previously Plummer Rodis and now partly occupied by Loch Fyne fish restaurant) and the former Elim church (now a pub) in the Lanes. Many other fine houses in Kemp Town along Marine Parade are theirs, and they also built part of Regency Square.

Above: Wilds's tomb in St Nicholas churchyard.

Below: Elim church.

Wilds died aged 71 and is buried in St Nicholas churchyard in Dyke Road. His tomb is covered with punning ammonite motifs and was probably designed by his son Amon Henry Wilds, who was responsible for the Royal Albion Hotel, Sillwood House, the Unitarian church in New Road and the Victoria Fountain in Old Steine.

840 Dennis Trident – carried the name since delivery in April 2000 on METRO Line 49. Renamed Ian Caldwell during April 2001, then back to Amon Wilds.

864 KING WILLIAM IV

Known as the Sailor King, he came to the throne late in life after his brother, George IV, died in 1830. William visited Brighton many times when he was Duke of Clarence, and he kept on the connection once he became king. On his first official visit as monarch in 1830 a floral arch 50ft high was displayed at the northern entrance of the Royal Pavilion.

William stayed in the resort for part of every year until his death in 1837, and he would been seen walking in the town with Queen Adelaide. Sometimes he would go to Kemp Town or visit the Chain Pier. He also continued the development of the Pavilion, calling it the Royal Palace, Brighton: a room in the Pavilion is named after him. He is reputed to have fathered several children by sundry mistresses, but as none of them was legitimate he was succeeded by his

niece Victoria. The Pavilion fell into disfavour during the reign of Queen Victoria, who disliked its lack of privacy. She decided to stay at Osborne House on the Isle of Wight instead.

The North Gate of the Royal Pavilion.

864 Dennis Trident – carried name since delivery in April 2001 on METRO Line 5.

862 JAMES WILLIAMSON

James Williamson could have been just another chemist, but thanks to his association with George Albert Smith he went down in history. The two men, operating late in the nineteenth century, were among the early pioneers of film. Smith had a studio in St Ann's Well Garden and Williamson had a shop in Church Road, Hove.

Born in Scotland in 1855, Williamson moved south as a young man and was in Hove by 1886. Both he and Smith were members of Hove Camera Club, and Williamson was happy to give exhibitions. He went full time into films in 1898, making 39 of them in one year alone.

Smith and Williamson made short silent films which were innovative in that they had a story line. Some were comic, too. Williamson became a major producer in the first decade of the twentieth century, with a thriving

The shop in Church Road.

export trade to the USA. He made 50 films a year in the decade from 1902 and eventually moved to London after establishing a works in Cambridge Grove, Hove. In the capital he ran a successful business, manufacturing film apparatus and developing film. He died in Richmond in 1933.

862 Dennis Trident – carried name since delivery in March 2001 on METRO Line 5.

774 BOB WILSON

At Brighton & Hove's Awards Evening in 2002 staff had the chance to bid for the opportunity of having their name on a bus. The event raised more than £1,700 for charity. Bob Wilson was a driver at our Conway Street depot.

774 Scania Cityzen – carried name from April to June 2002.

863 JOHN WISDEN

Born in Brighton in 1826, John Wisden soon became one of the foremost cricketers of the day. Playing in a match between the North and South in 1850, he took all 10 wickets and is still the only man in history to have achieved this feat by bowling all his victims. Wisden, a fearsome fast bowler, played for Sussex between 1845 and 1863, and for many years there was a sports shop in Duke Street

which had family connections. His greatest claim to fame was founding, in 1864, the almanac which still bears his name today. Known as the cricketers' bible, *Wisden* contains every detail anyone could wish to know about the game – and a great deal more besides.

863 Dennis Trident – carried name since delivery in March 2001 on METRO Line 5.

20 SIR NORMAN WISDOM

The famous actor/comedian and star of theatre, film, radio, cabaret and television was a director of Brighton & Hove Albion and has many connections with the city. He retired in 2004 – at the age of 90.

20 Dennis Dart – carried name from September 1999 on METRO Line 7. Originally Norman Wisdom: 'Sir' added in January 2002 after the award of his knighthood. Name stayed until May 2004 when the bus was repainted into new livery.

636 GRACE EYRE WOODHEAD

This pioneer in mental health started her work at the end of the nineteenth century with a scheme to arrange holiday homes in Brighton for London children who had special needs. It was almost unheard of in those days to take people with mental handicaps out of care and into the community. As a result of her work the Guardianship Society was formed. In 1988 the name was changed to the Grace Eyre Foundation.

Miss Woodhead died in 1935, but her work lives on in the city in many ways. Today the Foundation deals with adults, rather than children, who have learning difficulties, and it gives them care and support. This work began in 1914 with a day centre in Brighton offering industrial training, and in 1950 moved to Hove, taking over an old Methodist church in Old Shoreham Road, which became the Avondale Centre. In 1998 the Foundation opened a second day centre in Hove for elderly people with learning difficulties, this time in Walsingham Road.

The Avondale Centre.

636 Scania Omnidekka – carried name since delivery in February 2004 on METRO Line 1.

768 ADAM TRIMINGHAM

The criteria for having a bus name is now firmly established: the individual has not only made a significant contribution to the life of the city but is dead. It was a great pleasure to make an exception for our good friend Adam Trimingham for the first year of his well earned retirement as senior reporter at the *Argus* in August 2004.

Adam has taken a keen interest in the bus name project since its inception and has been a great help to us each year, sifting through all the many suggestions which are regularly sent in to ensure that each batch of new buses has a balanced list of newsworthy names. He has also spent many hours researching and writing this book.

Adam is a journalist held in high esteem by all whom he met during his distinguished career. His ability to communicate his extensive knowledge of the city and surrounding area has left a lasting legacy of well informed citizens with a better grasp of the many issues facing the community. Luckily he is continuing to write in his retirement, and we hope his bus name will be a reminder to everyone during the forthcoming year of the excellent work he contributed to the city while he was at the *Argus*.

**768 Scania Cityzen –
carried name since
August 2004.**

INDEX

INDEX